Speaking Games

By Jason Anderson

DELTA PUBLISHING

Acknowledgements

I would like to thank the following individuals and schools for their assistance in trialling the material herein:

The many teachers in the towns of Keningau, Tambunan and Tenom in Sabah, Malaysia who tried out these games with great enthusiasm and offered feedback and input into their development; Fiona McGarry and her learners; the teachers and students at Rose of York Language School, London; David Foster and the teachers and students of British Study Centres, London; the teachers and students of both London School of English and Wimbledon School of English.

All the images on the cover of this book depict learners and teachers at Rose of York Language School and Training 4 TEFL, London, to whom I am grateful for permission to use the images.

I would also like to thank everybody who has provided positive feedback on my two previous photocopiable resource books for DELTA Publishing - *Role Plays for Today* and *Teamwork* - and their encouragement to write something new.

I would like to acknowledge Mario Rinvolucri's creative influence and his game *Grammar Auction* as the inspiration for my rather more cynical *Lie Auction*. Jill Hadfield's many *Communication Games* books have also been an inspiration for this collection.

I would also like to thank Nick Boisseau of DELTA Publishing for seeing potential in my proposal, Fiona McGarry as my patient editor, Nick Asher the designer and Tom Pemberton-Parker for his illustrations.

Finally, I would like to thank the Bornean Banded Pitta *Hydrornis schwaneri*, the Rufous-bellied Tit *Melaniparus rufiventris* and the Wattled Ibis *Bostrychia carunculata* for obvious reasons.

Published by
DELTA PUBLISHING
Quince Cottage
Hoe Lane
Peaslake
Surrey GU5 9SW
England
www.deltapublishing.co.uk

Text © Jason Anderson 2014
Design and illustration © Delta Publishing 2014
First published 2014
ISBN 978-1-905085-98-9

All rights reserved. No part of this publication may be reproduced, stored in a retrieval system or transmitted in any form or by any means, electronic, mechanical, photocopying, recording or otherwise, without the prior permission of the publishers.

Edited by Fiona McGarry
Designed by Nick Asher
Illustrated by Tom Pemberton-Parker
Printed in China by RR Donnelley

Contents

Section 1: Board Games		Levels			Language Focus	
Page		B1	B2	C1	Sub-skills & Functions	Grammar Ⓖ & Lexis Ⓛ
10	What's the Topic?	✓	✓	✓	• improvising short topic-based turns • speaking fluently without pausing • asking questions spontaneously	Ⓖ spoken discourse markers and conjunctions Ⓛ various topics
12	Opinion Olympics		✓	✓	• expressing opinions • agreeing and disagreeing • providing reasons	Ⓛ expressions for giving opinions, agreeing and disagreeing
14	Supermarket Scramble	✓	✓		• giving personal information • describing dishes, food and diets • naming items in a list	Ⓖ present simple Ⓛ food and shopping Ⓛ health and diets
16	Haunted Hotel	✓	✓	✓	• narrating a story • describing people, places and things	Ⓖ past simple and past continuous Ⓛ adjectives to describe people, places and things
18	Question Maze	✓	✓	✓	• formulating questions • recalling recent events • describing future arrangements	Ⓖ question forms Ⓖ *going to* and present continuous for future plans / arrangements Ⓖ past simple
20	Alphabet Race	✓	✓	✓	• naming items within a category • describing a hobby, place, the weather, etc. • expressing personal preferences	Ⓛ free time activities / hobbies or Ⓛ countries of the world / travel
22	Comperlative Maze	✓	✓	✓	• comparing people, places and things • discussing the validity of a statement	Ⓖ comparative structures Ⓖ superlative structures Ⓛ science and technology Ⓛ geography
24	Animal Comparatives	✓	✓		• comparing qualities • describing abilities	Ⓖ comparative adjectives and adverbs Ⓖ *as* + adjective + *as* structures Ⓛ animals
26	Word Formation Maze		✓	✓	• transforming words from one part of speech to another • producing example sentences spontaneously	Ⓛ parts of speech Ⓛ suffixes
28	Sport Busters	✓	✓	✓	• describing rules and conditions • expressing obligation and prohibition	Ⓖ modal verbs of obligation and prohibition Ⓛ sports
30	Phrasal Verb Addiction		✓	✓	• responding quickly to questions	Ⓛ phrasal verbs
32	Personality Connections	✓	✓	✓	• describing characteristics and personality	Ⓛ adjectives to describe personality
35	Description Bingo	✓	✓		• describing appearance • asking *yes / no* questions	Ⓖ *have got / have* Ⓖ adjective order Ⓛ features of the face

© Delta Publishing 2014   SPEAKING GAMES by Jason Anderson

Page	Section 2: Card Games	B1	B2	C1	Sub-skills & Functions	Grammar ⓖ & Lexis ⓛ
38	Advice Rummy	✓	✓		• giving advice • thinking of creative solutions to problems	ⓖ modal verbs and other structures for giving advice
40	Grammar Gym	✓	✓		• conjugating verbs accurately at speed	ⓖ all tenses / aspects that your learners already know
42	Say the Right Thing	✓	✓	✓	• responding appropriately to good and bad news • using intonation and body language to convey meaning	ⓖ so do I / me too ⓛ spoken attention signals
45	'Both' & 'Neither' Snap	✓	✓	✓	• thinking creatively under time pressure • drawing comparisons • challenging the validity of a statement	ⓖ both and neither ⓖ have to for obligation ⓛ occupations
46	Just a Minute!	✓	✓	✓	• monitoring accuracy while speaking fluently • peer-correcting errors	ⓛ spoken fillers ⓛ spoken hedging expressions
47	Dragons' Lair		✓	✓	• pitching an original business idea • responding to probing questions	ⓖ 1st conditional structures ⓖ 2nd conditional structures ⓛ business and finance
50	Original Opinions	✓	✓	✓	• expressing opinions • agreeing and disagreeing • describing conditions	ⓖ zero conditional structures ⓛ expressions for giving opinions
52	The Thing about Cleft Sentences…		✓	✓	• commenting on a topic / issue • expressing opinions • providing supporting arguments • adding emphasis	ⓖ cleft sentences ⓖ it as a preparatory subject ⓖ complex sentences
54	Pros and Cons Dice	✓	✓	✓	• generating ideas quickly • challenging an idea	ⓖ comparative structures
55	Question Poker	✓	✓	✓	• recalling specific information accurately • expressing feelings and desires	ⓖ verb patterns ⓖ future forms
56	Regrets		✓	✓	• expressing regret and/or criticism • peer-correcting formal errors	ⓖ 3rd conditional structures ⓖ mixed conditional structures ⓖ should have + past participle ⓖ I wish… / If only… structures

SPEAKING GAMES by Jason Anderson © Delta Publishing 2014

Page	Section 3: Secrets & Lies	B1	B2	C1	Sub-skills & Functions	Grammar (G) & Lexis (L)
57	True Secrets		✓	✓	• asking and answering improvised questions • inventing information quickly	(G) question forms (L) personal information
60	Truth or Lie	✓	✓	✓	• making short, unprepared speaking turns • inventing information quickly • analysing a spoken text critically	(G) past simple (G) reported speech
62	Tag on the Back	✓	✓	✓	• making guesses • using intonation to sound friendly • correcting misconceptions	(G) question tags (G) 'same way' question tags (L) use of *actually* to correct factual errors
64	Question Taboo	✓	✓	✓	• paraphrasing • reformulating an idea	(G) present simple tense (L) personal information
66	Truth Mingle	✓	✓	✓	• identifying things in common • speculating on possible future events • enquiring about future plans • describing future plans	(G) future perfect (G) future continuous (G) present continuous / *going to* for future arrangements / intentions
68	Gotcha!	✓	✓		• improvising questions • leading a conversation	(G) question forms (L) food and drink (or any other lexical area)
70	Secret Sentences	✓	✓	✓	• agreeing and disagreeing • challenging someone's opinion • eliciting agreement	(L) spoken discourse markers
72	This Weekend	✓	✓	✓	• describing future plans and arrangements • interviewing someone	(G) *going to* for future plans (G) present continuous for future arrangements
74	Passive Porkies	✓	✓	✓	• improvising responses to questions • describing recent events • asking follow-up questions	(G) passive forms (present simple, past simple, present perfect) (G) question forms
76	Kangaroo Court		✓	✓	• justifying past actions • thinking creatively • interrogating a suspect • responding to accusations	(G) narrative tenses (L) crime and courtroom
78	Would I lie to you?	✓	✓	✓	• asking questions / interrogating • describing past experiences • recalling an anecdote	(G) narrative tenses (G) present perfect for life experience
80	Lie Auction	✓	✓	✓	• describing abilities, past events and habits • hypothesising about possible abilities, events and habits • asking questions	(any or all of the following) (G) present perfect for life experience (G) *can / could* for ability (G) *used to* for past habits

Page	Section 4: Puzzles & Challenges	Levels B1 B2 C1	Sub-skills & Functions	Grammar (G) & Lexis (L)
82	Word Countdown	✓ ✓ ✓	• manipulating sentence syntax at speed • connecting ideas creatively	(G) sentence formation (G) relative clauses (G) past tenses (G) linking expressions
83	Riddle Race	✓ ✓ ✓	• lateral / creative thinking • explaining an abstract idea	(G) conjunctions for explaining and justifying
86	Who wants to be an 'Idiom'aire?	✓ ✓ ✓	• predicting the meaning of unfamiliar lexis • providing reasons for choices • coming to an agreement	(L) idioms
88	How to Rob a Bank	✓ ✓ ✓	• describing sequences of events • making suggestions • justifying ideas and opinions	(G) modal verbs of possibility (G) 1st and 2nd conditional structures (L) crime and courtroom
90	The Key to the Problem	✓ ✓ ✓	• describing procedures in detail • describing diagrams or movements • making presentations • justifying a suggestion	(L) verbs of movement and action (L) tools
92	Third Person Challenge	✓ ✓	• accurately manipulating form when responding to questions	(G) 3rd person of present simple tense
94	Be Reasonable	✓ ✓ ✓	• providing reasons • disputing and justifying opinions • describing hypothetical situations	(G) *would*, *could* and *should* to describe hypothetical situations (L) linkers of reason and purpose
95	Needs Analysis Challenge	✓ ✓ ✓	• describing needs, preferences and interests • discussing and coming to a consensus • expressing opinions	(L) education (L) language learning
98	Dopey Dave	✓ ✓ ✓	• telling a story • describing events in detail	(G) narrative tenses (G) time expressions (L) shopping (L) relationships
101	Short Answer Challenge	✓ ✓	• asking *yes / no* questions • eliciting a chosen answer to a question • providing short answers to questions	(G) auxiliary verbs including modal auxiliary verbs (G) *yes / no* questions (G) short answers
102	Crime Scene Investigation	✓ ✓ ✓	• describing an image in detail • making inferences • speculating about past events	(G) present continuous (G) *there is / are* (G) modals of probability (present and past) (G) past simple and continuous (L) clothing
104	Guess the Question	✓ ✓	• making predictions • giving personal information	(G) question forms (L) personal interests
106	What a Coincidence!	✓ ✓ ✓	• speculating • linking ideas together • formulating a hypothesis • narrating a story	(G) narrative tenses (G) past modals of deduction (G) time sequencers
108	Guess the Story	✓ ✓ ✓	• making guesses • asking questions	(G) present continuous (G) narrative tenses (G) time sequencers

Contents

Resource bank

Page	
112	Comparative and Superlative prompt cards
113	Country question cards
114	Free Time Activity question cards
115	Job cards
116	Opinion cards
117	Personalisation question cards
118	Phrasal Verb question cards
119	Pros and Cons cards
120	Reason cards
121	Regret cards
122	Three Stories
123	Topic cards (easy)
124	Topic cards (challenging)
125	Word cards

Indexes

Page	
126	Grammar / Structure
127	Topic / Vocabulary
128	Function / Speaking sub-skill

© Delta Publishing 2014   SPEAKING GAMES by Jason Anderson

Introduction

... what great difference is there between 'work' and 'play' when concentration is sharply focused and the learner's energies stretched to the full?

W. R. Lee, Language Teaching Games and Contests, 1965

I love playing games. So do my learners - and it sounds as though Lee's did too, many years before the communicative approach to language teaching became the predominant methodology. Given the number of authors who, since then, have recognised the importance of play in language learning (e.g. Rinvolucri 1995, Cook 2000, Gonzalez-Davies 2004, Wright et al. 2006), it may seem surprising that, even in the publishing world, there is still a reluctance to talk about them as 'games'. Within the wide range of resource materials available for English language teachers today, the very fact that the name Speaking Games was available for this book reflects this reluctance.

Despite the wealth of research that has taken place into second language acquisition since Lee wrote his book, there is still concern in many quarters that games, while suitable for the end of the lesson, or a break from 'study', can't really constitute the core of that study. I suppose the fact that this book is a resource book (i.e. for the fun bit at the end of the lesson) supports this opinion. However, I hope that my attempt to create a clear link between play and language learning outcomes may convince some of the sceptics that play can and should be central to the language learning process for adults, as it has always been for children. To this end, I have described functions, sub-skills, grammatical and lexical areas practised in each game in both the Teacher's preparation notes for the game and the Contents at the start of the book. Many of the games in this book can be used diagnostically (to check for prior knowledge of an area of language), for practice after a presentation, and for revision. In addition, some of the games can be used as icebreakers, rapport builders and even needs analysis tools (see page 95 – Needs Analysis Challenge).

Games have many benefits, both for language learning and cognitive development. Here are a few:

- games are enjoyable and likely to boost intrinsic motivation for language learning;
- interaction within games often involves authentic communication, especially when learners debate rules, manage turn-taking, and evaluate their performance;
- the challenge to communicate successfully during a game often leads to negotiation of meaning, an important part of language learning;
- games are inherently task-based - the task is to win;
- games often involve repetition of specific structures, something that is likely to promote 'chunking' of language and acquisition;
- the games in this book involve a number of higher-order thinking skills, including creating, evaluating and analysing;
- games provide opportunities to promote greater learner autonomy, as learners manage their own interaction and game play;
- through playing games learners acquire social skills, especially useful if a narrowly-focused education has denied them the opportunity to do this fully during their school years.

What makes an activity a speaking game?

While selecting activities for this book, I chose to define a Speaking Game as *an activity in which learners use spoken language in order to reach a predefined goal in competition with one another*. Of course, competition means there are always winners and losers, and for some learners, losing a game can be demotivating, so teacher discretion is always recommended, especially with teenagers. However, this competitive edge is also likely to inspire more animated interaction and push learners to perform to the best of their abilities. It also leads to more authentic language use around the game itself as learners discuss rules, negotiate scores and build more colourful relationships that lead to further interaction. Regarding the use of 'spoken language', I have chosen to include activities that focus on meaningful, spontaneous language use alongside activities that focus more on aspects of form and accuracy, both of which have a role to play in language learning.

Of course, there will always be some learners (some classes even) who need to be reminded that the game itself is just a means to an end, and that winning the game is less important than learning language, so it's a good idea to make the language learning aims of the game clear during the activity introduction. If you like to give prizes or privileges for winners, you could also offer a prize for 'best language use' or even 'fair play'.

How to use the book

Contents and indexes

You can find the game you need using either the Contents (where you can browse games according to category), or the three Indexes at the back of the book (grammar/structure, topic/vocabulary and function/sub skill). The games have been categorised as follows:

- **Board Games:** includes games for which there is a photocopiable game board. Individual counters and sometimes dice are usually necessary to play these games. Some teachers prefer to enlarge the boards to A3 size when copying, although all can be played at A4 size as well.
- **Card Games:** includes games in which learners use cards in some way. There are traditional card game formats such as Snap and Rummy, prompt cards for mingle activities and topic cards for discussion games.
- **Secrets and Lies:** includes games in which learners may have to guess each other's secrets or deceive each other. Especially with this latter type of game where learners have to separate truth from lies, some learners may need a little encouragement and a demonstration to see that lying can be a creative, enjoyable form of play.
- **Puzzles and Challenges:** includes a wider variety of activities, such as story-based games, peer challenge activities and problem solving activities.

Teacher's notes

Teacher's notes are provided for each game, but these are kept to a minimum, describing preparation (usually just copying and sometimes cutting up) and procedure in class. Some games require resources from the Resource bank at the back of the book; if so, this is clearly stated under Preparation.

The Teacher's notes also include any useful additional information, tips or ideas, and the Variations section which suggests possible alternative ways to use the materials (see below).

Rules of the game - instructing made easy!

The majority of the games include a Rules of the game section (a few have a Worksheet instead) which has been written for learners to read themselves. This provides them with an authentic reading opportunity as part of the activity, and comprehension is demonstrated (or not) through how they play the game. Language in the texts has been carefully graded so that the instructions are easy to understand at the required levels. After learners have read the rules, double check understanding with a few instruction check questions, or if appropriate, a demonstration with one group of learners while the others observe.

Learner autonomy during game play

Once they have grasped the basic idea of a game, more experienced learners may want to adapt the game to suit their preferences. This may include making it non-competitive, changing the rules of game play, or using different interaction patterns (individual players, pairs or teams). If this works for them while also achieving your intended learning outcomes, there's no need to stick religiously to the rules.

Adapting the games

All good teachers adapt materials as part of the planning and preparation process. Only you know what works with your learners, so feel free to be creative. The Variations in the teacher's notes are only a starting point for adaptation. Some teachers like to simplify or to scaffold learning, others to increase the complexity or the challenge. A number of the games that have been designed to practise specific areas of language can easily be adapted to practise alternative areas. For example, in Lie Auction (page 80), learners can be encouraged to focus on almost any area of grammar or lexis.

A number of games involve learners talking about topics, such as Alphabet Race (page 20), Gotcha (page 68) and What's the Topic? (page 10). For games like these, you can add or substitute topics that have recently come up in class.

Resource bank

The cards in the Resource bank are designed for use with a number of different games and constitute useful general resources for teachers to draw upon when needed. These include Topic cards, Free Time Activity question cards, Job cards, Opinion cards and Pros and Cons cards. If you have the opportunity, you may want to laminate these cards as they lend themselves to a number of other activities in class.

Happy playing!

References

Cook, G. (2000) *Language Play, Language Learning* Oxford: Oxford University Press

González Davies, M. (2004) *Multiple Voices in the Translation Classroom - Activities, tasks and projects* Amsterdam: John Benjamins Publishing

Lee, W. R. (1965) *Language Teaching Games and Contests* Oxford: Oxford University Press

Rinvolucri, M. (1995) *Grammar Games – Cognitive, affective and drama activities for EFL students* Cambridge: Cambridge University Press

Wright, A., Betteridge, D. and Buckby, M. (2006) *Games for Language Learning Third Edition* Cambridge: Cambridge University Press

What's the topic?

Time	30–45 minutes
Interaction	Groups of 3–5 learners
Level	B1 (Intermediate) to C1 (Advanced)

Language areas practised

Sub-skills and Functions

- improvising short, topic-based speaking turns
- speaking fluently without pausing
- asking questions spontaneously

Grammar and Lexis

- spoken discourse markers and conjunctions (*also, and another thing, because,* etc.)
- various topics

Preparation

Photocopy the **Rules of the game**, the **Game board** and the **Topic cards** from pages 123–124 of the Resource bank (one of each per group). Choose the 'easy' topic cards for lower level learners and the 'challenging' cards for higher levels. Cut up the Topic cards as indicated. Players need one counter each (e.g. coins), one dice and one timer (e.g. a mobile phone) per group.

Notes

Before players begin, draw their attention to the first 'If…' rule to highlight the importance of listening and monitoring each other's language during the game.

Variations

- Instead of using the Topic cards, learners prepare for the game by writing a range of topics directly in the squares on the board (e.g. *Speak for a minute about … the party last night*). This enables them to personalise the topics to their interests and shared knowledge. Allow an extra 10 minutes for this.

What's the topic?   Rules of the game

Preparation

Play in groups of 3-5. Each group needs a **Game board**, a set of **Topic cards**, a dice, a timer (e.g. mobile phone) and some counters (e.g. coins). Place the Topic cards face down on the board. Each player places their counter on **Start**, ready to begin.

How to play

Take turns to roll the dice and move. When you land on a square, follow the instructions. For example: *Speak for 1 minute about…* (the topic on the card).

How to win

The first player to reach **Finish** wins the game.

If...

- If the square says: '*Speak for 30 seconds about…*' or '*Speak for 1 minute about…*', you take a Topic card and speak for this time on the topic without pausing or repeating any ideas.
- If the square says: '*Say 1 sentence about…*', you take a Topic card and say one sentence about this topic.
- If the card says: '*Ask 1/2/3 questions about…*' you take a Topic card and ask questions to other players on this topic, who should answer.
- If the card says: '*Go forward/back 1/2/3 spaces*', you should do this and then follow the instructions on the new square you land on.
- If you cannot carry out the instruction, you go back to your previous square.

What's the topic? — Game board

Section 1: Board Games

FINISH | Ask 3 questions about… | Speak for 1 minute about… | Go back 3 spaces | Speak for 1 minute about…

Ask 2 questions about…

Go back 2 spaces

WHAT'S THE TOPIC?

Ask 2 questions about… | Speak for 1 minute about… | Say 1 sentence about… | Go forward 1 space | Speak for 30 seconds about…

Speak for 30 seconds about…

Go back 3 spaces

PUT THE TOPIC CARDS HERE

Say 1 sentence about… | Go forward 1 space | Speak for 30 seconds about… | Ask 2 questions about… | Say 1 sentence about…

Go back 2 spaces

Go forward 1 space

WHAT'S THE TOPIC?

START | Say 1 sentence about… | Speak for 30 seconds about… | Speak for 1 minute about… | Ask 1 question about…

© Delta Publishing 2014 — SPEAKING GAMES by Jason Anderson

Opinion Olympics

Time	20–40 minutes
Interaction	Groups of 3–6 learners
Level	B2 (Upper Intermediate) to C1 (Advanced)

Language areas practised

Sub-skills and Functions

- expressing opinions
- agreeing and disagreeing
- providing reasons

Grammar and Lexis

- expressions for giving opinions, agreeing and disagreeing

Preparation

Photocopy the **Rules of the game**, the **Game board** and the **Opinion cards** from page 116 of the Resource bank (one of each per group). Remove any Opinion cards that you feel may be unsuitable for your learners. Cut up the Opinion cards as indicated. Players need one counter each (e.g. coins) and one dice per group.

If appropriate, check usage of the agreeing and disagreeing gambits around the Game board such as *The truth is …* and *Another reason why people …*

Notes

The learner who begins the game should respond to the opinion on the Current card, unless he lands on '*NEW CARD Do you agree?*'. For the rest of the game, the learners should be agreeing/disagreeing with the previously voiced opinion, rather than the opinion on the Current card. This encourages them to listen to each other and interact naturally using the gambits around the board.

Variations

- Players create their own Opinion cards before they start playing. It takes an extra 10 minutes, but leads to more animated conversations.

Opinion Olympics — Rules of the game

Preparation

Play in groups of 3-6. Each group needs a Game board, a set of **Opinion cards**, a dice and some counters (e.g. coins). Place the Opinion cards face down on the board. Turn over the top card and place it on the Current card square. Each player places their counter on **START** to begin.

How to play

Take turns to roll the dice and move around the board. When you land on a square you react to an opinion and give a reason. Your reaction will depend on the square you land on, *Agree, Disagree,* etc. Make sure you are familiar with all the expressions surrounding the board before you begin as you will need them for expressing your opinions.

How to win

The first player to reach **FINISH** wins the game.

If...

- If you land on '*NEW CARD Do you agree?*', you turn over a new Opinion card and say whether you agree or not, providing a reason for your opinion.
- If you land on '*Disagree*', you should disagree with the last speaker and give a reason.
- If you land on '*Agree and add something*', you agree with the last speaker and provide an additional reason.
- If you land on '*Sit on the fence*', you express a balanced opinion that acknowledges both sides of the argument.
- If you can't think of a reason for your opinion, you go back to your previous position and wait your next turn!

SPEAKING GAMES by Jason Anderson © Delta Publishing 2014

Opinion Olympics — Game board

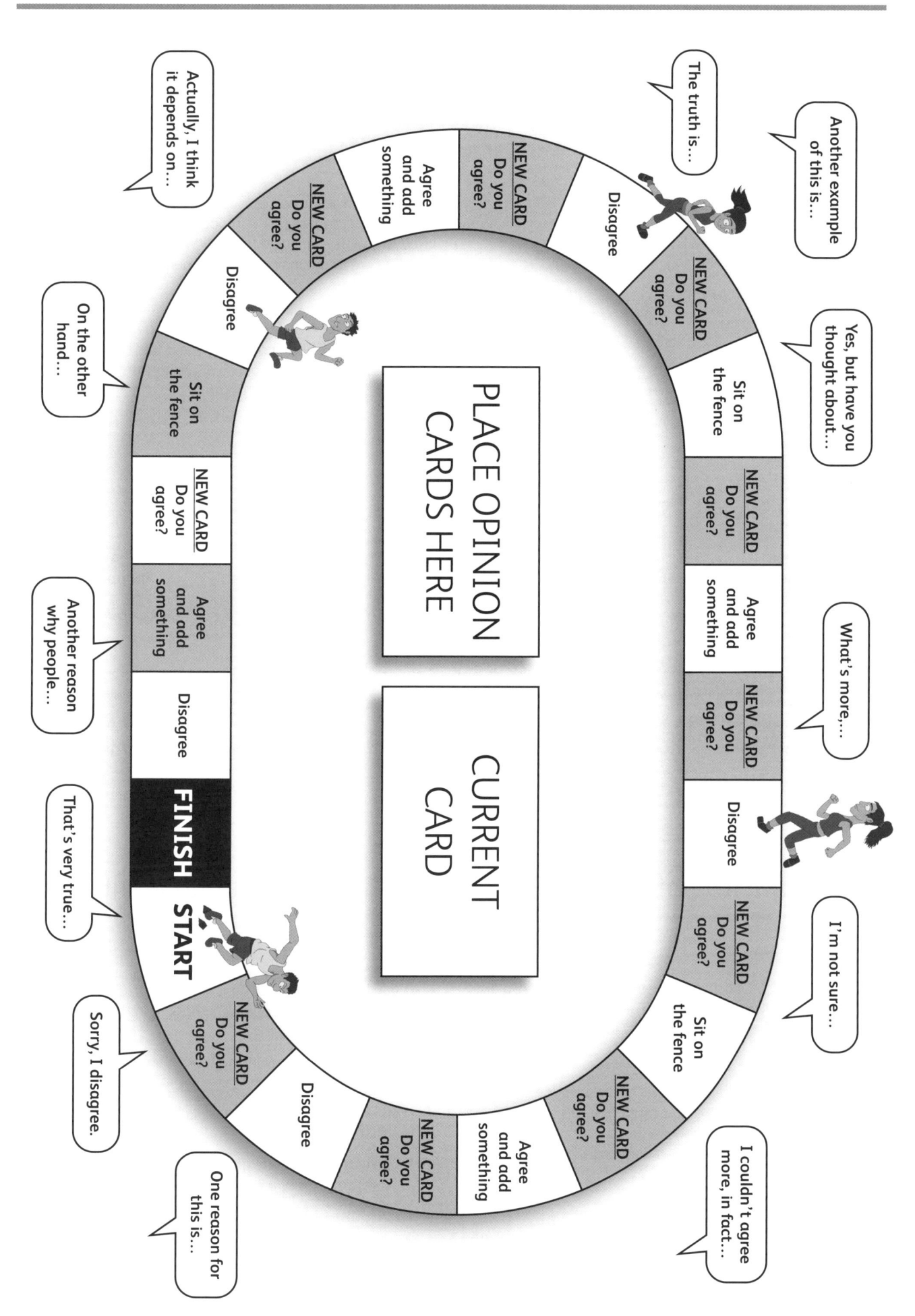

Section 1: Board Games

Board spaces (around the oval track):
- START / FINISH
- NEW CARD: Do you agree?
- Agree and add something
- Disagree
- Sit on the fence

Centre: **PLACE OPINION CARDS HERE** / **CURRENT CARD**

Speech bubbles:
- "Another example of this is…"
- "The truth is…"
- "Yes, but have you thought about…"
- "Actually, I think it depends on…"
- "On the other hand…"
- "What's more,…"
- "Another reason why people…"
- "I'm not sure…"
- "That's very true…"
- "I couldn't agree more, in fact,…"
- "Sorry, I disagree."
- "One reason for this is…"

© Delta Publishing 2014 — SPEAKING GAMES by Jason Anderson

Section 1: Board Games

Supermarket Scramble

Time	30–50 minutes
Interaction	Groups of 3–5 learners
Level	B1 (Intermediate) to B2 (Upper Intermediate)

Language areas practised

Sub-skills and Functions

- giving personal information
- describing dishes, food and diets
- naming items in a list

Grammar and Lexis

- present simple tense
- food and shopping
- health and diets

Preparation

Photocopy the **Rules of the game**, the **Game board** and the **Shopping lists** (one of each per group). Cut up the Shopping lists as indicated. Players need one counter each (e.g. coins) and one dice per group.

Notes

This is quite a skilful game as players choose which way to move in order to pick up the products they need. At lower levels, students may need to check with you about which products are found in which departments.

Variations

- **Lower Levels** – Begin by writing a range of food products from the five Shopping lists on the board along with the five departments. Learners work in pairs to categorise the foods and then play the game.

Supermarket Scramble – Shopping lists

Player A Shopping List	Player B Shopping List	Player C Shopping List	Player D Shopping List	Player E Shopping List
fresh onions	eggs	fresh croissants	a birthday cake	shower gel
pasta sauce	mint mouthwash	corn flakes	fresh lemons	fresh carrots
milk	chocolate biscuits	conditioner for dry hair	strawberry yoghurt	ice cream
oven chips	frozen lasagne	parmesan cheese	curry powder	fresh prawns
fresh tuna steaks	ripe bananas	fresh lettuce	fresh fillet steak	buns for hamburgers
loaf of wholemeal bread	a fresh turkey	frozen pizza	moisturising cream	peanut butter

---

Supermarket Scramble

Rules of the game

Preparation

Play in groups of 3-5. Each group needs a **Game board**, a dice, and a **Shopping list** and counters (e.g. coins) for each player. Each player places their counter on **ENTRANCE** to begin.

How to play

Take turns to roll the dice and move in any direction. You move the number of squares indicated. You can't turn around during a move or move diagonally. See the 'If…' rules for how to pick up products on your shopping list and what to do when you land on a square.

How to win

The first player to get to **CHECKOUT** with all the products on her list wins the game.

If…

- If you land on a department (e.g. 'Dairy', 'Toiletries'), you can collect any food products that are in this department. Cross them off your list.

- If you pass over a department but don't land on it, you can't collect any food.

- If you land on a question, answer the question or name the food.

- If you can't answer the question or name the food, you must return to your previous square.

- If you arrive at the Checkout and realise you've forgotten something, you must go back for it!

SPEAKING GAMES by Jason Anderson © Delta Publishing 2014

Supermarket Scramble

Game board

Supermarket Scramble!!!

Section 1: Board Games

ENTRANCE — START HERE

- What food do you need to buy this week?
- How often do you usually do the shopping?
- What's your favourite food?
- **DAIRY** — milk, cheese, eggs, butter, margarine, yoghurt, etc.
- Name 3 things that we shouldn't eat too much of in a healthy diet.
- How healthy is your shopping list?
- Name 3 foods you can't live without.
- Do you prefer shopping in supermarkets or fresh food markets?
- What did you eat when you last went to a restaurant?

FRESH FRUIT & VEG. — apples, oranges, potatoes, tomatoes, mushrooms, salad, flowers, etc.

- Name 7 vegetables.
- What do you dislike most about supermarket shopping?
- How do you usually pay for your shopping?

CHECKOUT
- Have you got everything on your list?
- Have you ever tried to use a self-service checkout?

- Name 3 things you always buy when you do the shopping.
- **BREAD & BAKED PRODUCTS** — bread, buns, pastries, cakes, cookies, etc.
- How healthy is your diet?
- Name 6 fruit.
- How often does it usually take you to do the shopping?
- **FROZEN FOODS** — ice cream, ready meals, pizza, frozen vegetables, etc.
- What are the advantages of shopping in supermarkets?
- What are the ingredients of the most famous dish from your country?
- **TOILETRIES** — soap, shampoo, toothpaste, toilet paper, nappies, etc.
- Name 3 foods that you don't like.
- What is your favourite meal to prepare when guests visit you?
- What was the last meal you cooked?
- **MEAT & FISH** — chicken, lamb, sausages, beef, seafood, salmon, etc.
- Name 5 types of meat.
- **FOOD CUPBOARD** — rice, pasta, ingredients, sauces, crisps, spreads, biscuits, cereals, etc.
- What do you have in your fridge at the moment?

© Delta Publishing 2014

SPEAKING GAMES by Jason Anderson

Haunted Hotel

Time	30–45 minutes
Interaction	Groups of 3–5 learners
Level	B1 (Intermediate) to C1 (Advanced)

Language areas practised

Sub-skills and Functions

- narrating a story
- describing people, places and things

Grammar and Lexis

- past simple and past continuous tenses
- adjectives to describe people, places and things

Preparation

Photocopy the **Rules of the game** and the **Game board** (one of each per group). Players need one counter each (e.g. coins) and one dice per group. Before the game begins, read through *'The Story So Far'* with the learners (see Rules of the game). Make sure they understand that they should recount the story as a past event.

Notes

This game provides semi-controlled speaking practice of past simple and past continuous tenses. The degree of control will depend on the imagination and creativity of the learners. It could also provide inspiration for story writing, either for homework or in a future lesson.

Variations

- Learners move round as a team, using one counter only and flipping a coin instead of a dice – heads: one space – tails: two spaces.
- The learner on the right of the current player asks the question. If they get the question right, they get a bonus point.

Haunted Hotel — Rules of the game

Preparation

Play in groups of 3-5. Each group needs a **Game board**, a dice and some counters (e.g. coins). Each player places their counter on **START**, ready to begin.

The story so far...

Last year you saw an advert for a discount holiday, staying at a hotel in the country. So you made a booking that you regretted for the rest of your life! You are now going to tell the story while playing a game. Use your imagination to make it interesting and scary! Remember to tell the story in the past. Good luck!

How to play

Take turns to roll the dice and move around the board. You play the game as a team and try to tell a story that links together.

How to win

The first player to reach the **EXIT** wins!

If...

- If you land on a square with a question, first use the verbs in brackets to ask the question (using past simple and/or past continuous), and then answer the question.
- If you land on an image, describe it using past simple and/or past continuous.
- If you land on a *'secret staircase'* or a *'trap door'*, follow the arrow.
- If you land on the same square as another player, move forward one square.
- If you land on a square that somebody has already landed on, move forward one square.

Haunted Hotel — Game board

Section 1: Board Games

POWER CUT! GO BACK 2 SPACES	You ___ a knock on the door. What ___ next? (hear, happen)	*(skeleton)*	**SECRET STAIRCASE!**	What ___ while you ___ your bags? (happen, unpack)
You ___ to the restaurant for dinner. What ___ in the restaurant? (go, happen)	You ___ around. What ___ behind you? (turn, happen)	**POWER CUT! GO BACK 3 SPACES**	You ___ in the mirror. What ___ you ___? (look, see)	You ___ your room. Describe your room. (get to)
(zombie waiter)	**TRAP DOOR!**	**EXIT — YOU'RE SAFE! Now help your friends!**	*(portrait)*	What ___ in the main hall when you ___ through it? (happen, walk)
Describe the other guests. What ___ they ___? (eat)	*(ghost)*	**TRAP DOOR!**	What ___ when you ___ back to your room? (happen, get)	Describe the person who ___ the door. (open)
SECRET STAIRCASE!	You ___ down at your hands. What ___ you ___? (look, notice)	*(snake)*	**TRAP DOOR!**	*(vampire in coffin)*
What ___ you ___? What ___ they ___? (order, bring)	You ___ a cat. What ___ it ___? (see, do)	*(witch)*	You ___ out of the restaurant. What ___ next? (run, happen)	You ___ on the door. What ___ next? (knock, happen)
START	What ___ the weather like when you ___ the bus? (be, get off)	Describe the old hotel when you ___ it for the first time. (see)	*(bats and moon)*	What ___ as you ___ through the garden? (happen, walk)

© Delta Publishing 2014 — SPEAKING GAMES by Jason Anderson

Section 1: Board Games

Question Maze

Time	20–30 minutes
Interaction	Pairs
Level	B1 (Intermediate) to C1 (Advanced)

Language areas practised

Sub-skills and Functions
- formulating questions
- recalling recent events
- describing future arrangements

Grammar and Lexis
- question forms
- *going to* and present continuous for future plans / arrangements
- past simple

Preparation
Photocopy the **Rules of the game** and the **Question Maze** (one of each per pair).

Notes
Question Maze provides semi-controlled practice of formulating questions. It's a useful 'half-way' stage to free question formation as it both guides and challenges learners to be creative and ambitious, while also focussing on accuracy. Be aware that learners can get so wrapped up in formulating questions that they forget to answer each other's questions (see the final 'If…' rule).

Variations
- **Original Questions** – Instead of scoring points for using the squares, players score a point for each original question they can make. This leads to a lot of speaking practice as there are over 50 possible questions on the board!

Question Maze

Preparation
Play in pairs. Each pair needs a **Game board**, a piece of paper for keeping score and different coloured pens (to mark the questions). Flip a coin to decide who goes first.

How to play
Take it in turns to formulate questions by drawing a line from the start to the end of the question with your pen. You can move in any direction, but you can't jump a square.

what	who	where
tomorrow	are	when
you	going out	your friends

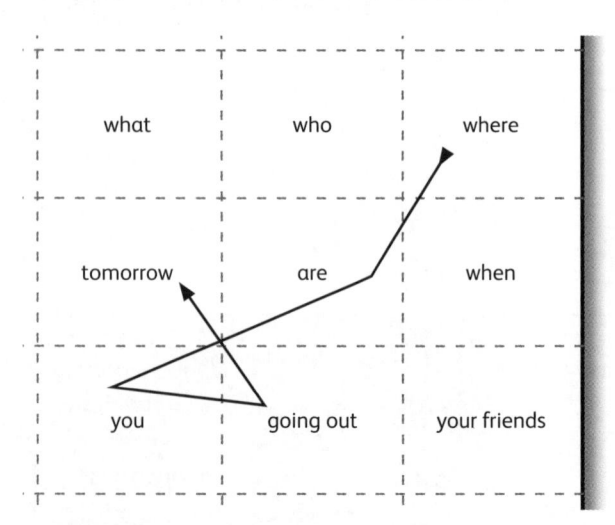

The example above forms the question: *Where are you going out tomorrow?* If you both agree the question is correct and logical, your partner should answer the question (see 'If…'

Rules of the game

rules). You score a point for each square used (five points in the example). Your partner now 'draws' a question. She can use squares that have already been used, but if so, she doesn't score any points for them. If you agree it's a good question, you answer it and your partner calculates her score. You now 'draw' your second question. Play continues until all the words on the board have been used.

How to win
The player with the highest score at the end of the game wins.

If…
- If you use a square that has already been used, you don't score a point for it.
- If you think your partner has made a grammatical mistake in the question, you can challenge it. If you are right, your partner loses a point and must try again. Ask the teacher if you disagree!
- If you challenge a question that is grammatically correct, you lose a point!
- If you forget to answer a question before taking your turn, you lose a point, but must still answer!

Question Maze

Game board

Section 1: Board Games

last night	this morning	yesterday	for breakfast	for dinner
learn	on the internet	do	last night	eat
buy	you	call	you	want to
yesterday	why	did	do	be
playing	are	what	who	where
learning	we	tomorrow	are	when
now	going to	you	going out	your friends
meet	do	posting	following	doing
after the lesson	this weekend	tomorrow	on Facebook or Twitter	tonight

© Delta Publishing 2014 SPEAKING GAMES by Jason Anderson

19

Alphabet Race

Time	20–30 minutes
Interaction	Groups of 3–4 learners
Level	B1 (Intermediate) to C1 (Advanced)

Language areas practised

Sub-skills and Functions

- naming items within a category
- describing a hobby, place, the weather, etc.
- expressing personal preferences

Grammar and Lexis

- free time activities

or

- countries of the world

Preparation

Photocopy the **Rules of the game** and the **Game board** (one of each per group). From the Resource bank, also photocopy either the **Country question cards** or the **Free Time Activity cards** (pages 113–114), depending on the language you want to practise. Cut up the Question cards as indicated.

Notes

This is a variation on a common category game that involves free speaking through both personalisation and general knowledge questions.

Variations

- **Other Categories** – This game can also be played with other categories (e.g. food, crimes, sports, etc.). You just need to add your own discussion questions.
- **Longer Game** – Players play by flipping a coin, rather than throwing a dice (heads: move one place forward – tails: move two places forward).

Alphabet Race — Rules of the game

Preparation

Play in groups of 3-4. Each group needs a **Game board**, a set of **Question cards**, a dice and some counters (e.g. coins). Place the Question cards face down on the board. Each player places their counter on **START**, ready to begin.

How to play

Your teacher will provide a category for the game (e.g. 'countries of the world' or 'free time activities'). Take turns to roll the dice and move. You must think of a word or phrase within the category (e.g. a country) that starts with the letter you land on. Then you pick up a Question card, read out the question and answer it about the word you have chosen. If you finish all the Question cards, collect them together, shuffle them and put them back on the board face down.

How to win

The first player to reach **FINISH** wins the game.

If...

- If you can't think of a word in a reasonable amount of time (e.g. 20 seconds), you must return to your previous square and wait for your next turn.
- If you can't answer a question, you must return to your previous square and wait for your next turn.
- If you think another player's answer to a general knowledge question is wrong, you can challenge it. Ask your teacher or use the Internet to check a challenge.
- If you land on a letter that another player has already landed on, you must think of a different word that starts with this letter.

Alphabet Race

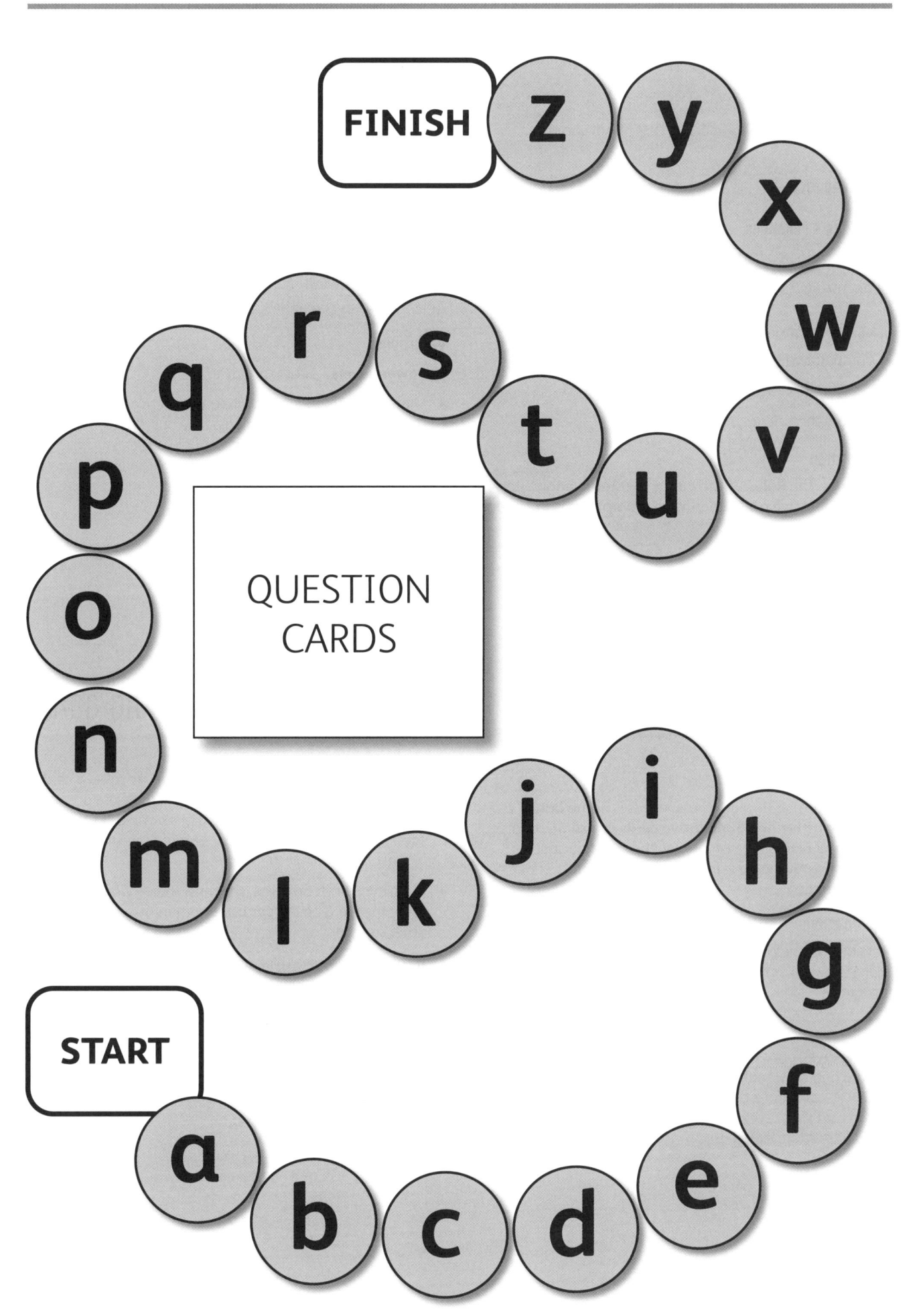

Game board

Section 1: Board Games

FINISH

z y x w v u t s r q p o n m l k j i h g f e d c b a

QUESTION CARDS

START

© Delta Publishing 2014

SPEAKING GAMES by Jason Anderson

21

Comperlative Maze

Time	20–45 minutes
Interaction	Groups of 3–4 learners
Level	B1 (Intermediate) to C1 (Advanced)

Language focus

Sub-skills & Functions
- comparing people, places and things
- discussing the validity of a statement

Grammar and Lexis
- comparative structures
- superlative structures
- geography, science, technology

Preparation

Photocopy the **Rules of the game**, the **Game board**, and the **Comparative and Superlative prompt cards** from page 112 of the Resource bank (one of each per group). Cut up as indicated. If you have a group of five learners, two can play as a pair team.

Notes

This game can be used to practise a range of comparative and superlative structures, including –er and –est adjectives, as + adjective + as, and more/most + adjective, depending on what the learners have studied.

Where appropriate, learners may choose to personalise or localise statements, for example:

'Luis has the oldest mobile phone in this class.'

As long as everyone agrees, this is fine.

Variations

- **Lower Levels** – Learners play in teams.
- **Higher Levels** – Players write the adjectives they use on the relevant squares. If an adjective has already been written on the board, players cannot use it.
- **Faster Game** – Play with dice.

Comperlative Maze — Rules of the game

Preparation

Play in groups of 3-4. Each group needs a **Game board**, a set of **Comparative and Superlative cards** and some counters. Each player places their counter on their starting square. Shuffle and put the cards in a pile, face down. You'll need one coin per group.

How to move

Player A flips the coin. If it lands on 'heads', he moves one square forward. If it lands on 'tails', he moves two squares forward.

If...

- If a player lands on a comparative square, she takes a card and must make a <u>true</u> statement using the word on the card and a comparative structure. For example, if the card says: 'sport', she could say: 'Football is a more popular sport than rugby.'
- If a player lands on a superlative square, he takes a card and must make a <u>true</u> statement using the word on the card and a superlative structure. For example, if the card says: 'mountain', he could say: 'Mount Everest is the highest mountain in the world.'
- If a player lands on a star, she must make two statements using the word on the card: one comparative and the other superlative.
- If the other players think a statement is not true, the player must try again.
- If a player cannot think of a statement, he must go back to his previous square.

How to win

The first player to get to their finish point is the winner.

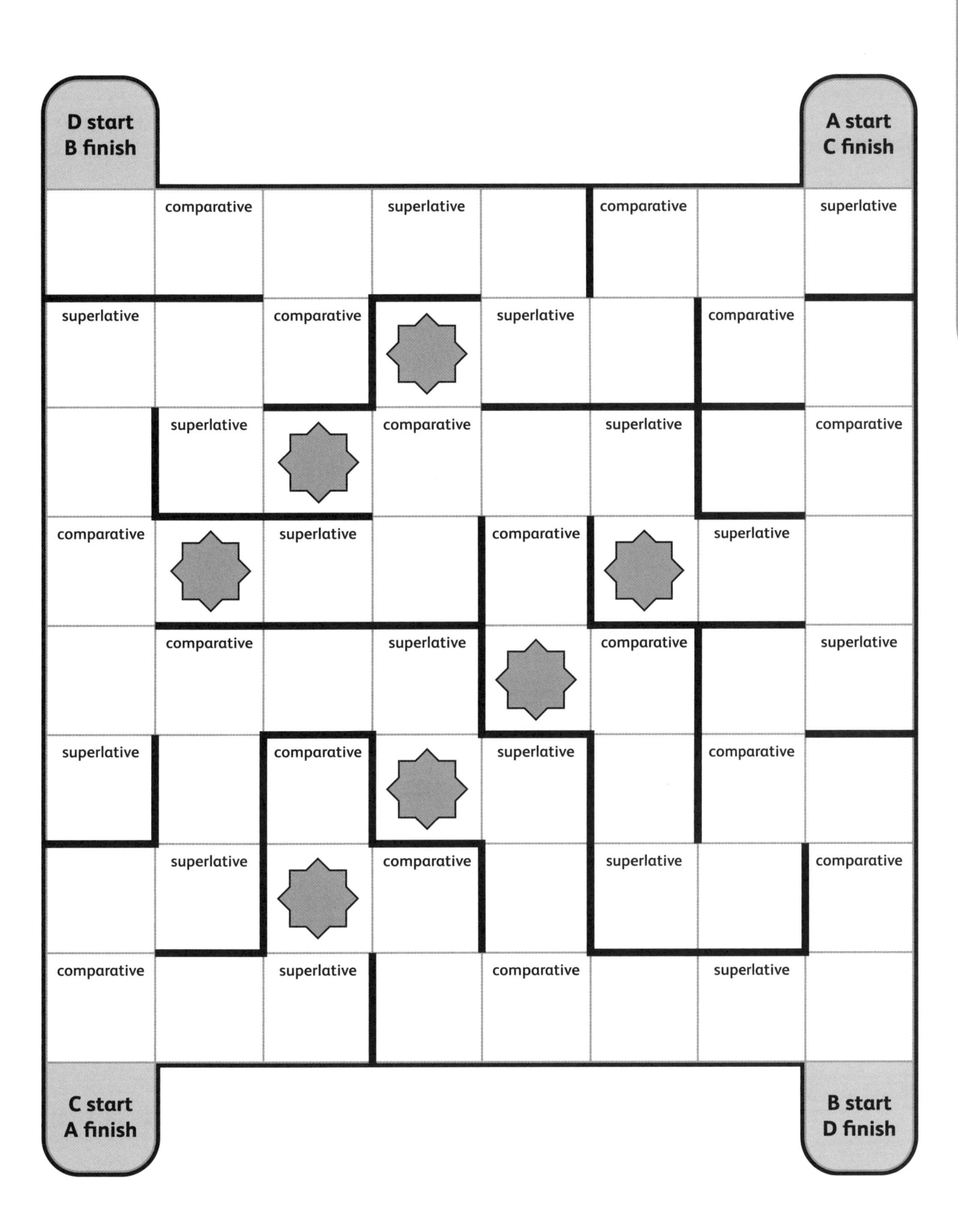

Comperlative Maze

Game board

Section 1: Board Games

| D start / B finish (top-left) | A start / C finish (top-right) |
| C start / A finish (bottom-left) | B start / D finish (bottom-right) |

Maze cells (row by row):

Row 1: _, comparative, _, superlative, _, comparative, _, superlative
Row 2: superlative, _, comparative, _, superlative, _, comparative, _
Row 3: _, superlative, _, comparative, _, superlative, _, comparative
Row 4: comparative, _, superlative, _, comparative, _, superlative, _
Row 5: _, comparative, _, superlative, _, comparative, _, superlative
Row 6: superlative, _, comparative, _, superlative, _, comparative, _
Row 7: _, superlative, _, comparative, _, superlative, _, comparative
Row 8: comparative, _, superlative, _, comparative, _, superlative, _

© Delta Publishing 2014 — SPEAKING GAMES by Jason Anderson

Section 1: Board Games

Animal Comparatives

Time	20–30 minutes
Interaction	Groups of 3–6 learners
Level	B1 (Intermediate) to B2 (Upper Intermediate)

Language areas practised

Sub-skills and Functions
- comparing qualities
- describing abilities

Grammar and Lexis
- comparative adjectives and adverbs
- *as* + adjective + *as* structures
- animals

Preparation
Photocopy the **Rules of the game** and the **Game board** (one of each per group). Players also need one counter each (e.g. coins).

Notes
Try to create larger groups of 4-6 learners if possible. This leads to more congestion in the centre of the board, and more tactical manoeuvring as a result. It doesn't matter which hexagons the players start from.

Variations
- **Higher Levels** – Learners aren't allowed to repeat an adjective already used. To ensure this rule is followed, players write down adjectives they've used on the sides of the Game board as they play.

Animal Comparatives   Rules of the game

Preparation
Play in groups of 3-6. Each group needs a **Game board** and some counters. Each player places their counter on one of the six starting points.

How to play
Take turns to move one hexagon in any direction. Compare the animal in the hexagon you have moved to with the animal in the hexagon you have just left. You can use either a comparative adjective (e.g. bigger), a comparative adverb, or an as + adjective + as structure. For example:

'An elephant is more intelligent than a fish.'

'A kangaroo can't run as quickly as a wolf.'

If the other players agree that the statement is true, you stay in your place. If they don't agree, you try again. If they don't agree a second time, you must go back to your original square and wait for your next turn.

How to win
The first player to get to their finishing point, on the other side of the board to their starting point, wins the game.

If...
- If other learners are in the hexagon where you want to move, you can't move there too, but should go around them.
- If players disagree about whether a statement is true, ask the teacher for his/her opinion – which is final.
- If you don't know the name of an animal, you miss a turn and your classmates or the teacher will tell you the name of the animal.

SPEAKING GAMES by Jason Anderson   © Delta Publishing 2014

Animal Comparatives

Game board

Section 1: Board Games

SPEAKING GAMES by Jason Anderson

© Delta Publishing 2014

Word Formation Maze

Time	15–30 minutes
Interaction	Pairs
Level	B2 (Upper Intermediate) to C1 (Advanced)

Language areas practised

Sub-skills and Functions

- transforming words from one part of speech to another
- producing example sentences spontaneously

Grammar and Lexis

- parts of speech
- suffixes

Preparation

Photocopy the **Game board**, the **Answer key** and the **Rules of the game** (one of each per pair). Separate the Answer key from the Game board and provide it at the end.

Notes

This game is obviously useful to learners studying for exams where knowledge of parts of speech and word transformations are tested. While the only 'in-game' spoken communication in this game is the example sentences, plenty of incidental conversation occurs as learners discuss and dispute possible forms and example sentences. Be on hand to help if learners disagree. Provide the answer key at the end.

Variations

- **High Levels** – Instead of thinking up example sentences, players think of a question to ask their opponent including the relevant part of speech.
- **Additional Rule** – If a learner completes a whole row, she gets an extra move.

Word Formation Maze — Rules of the game

Preparation

Play in pairs. Each pair needs two counters and you should use different coloured pens (black and blue is fine).

How to play

Players A and B start at different points. Take turns to move. You can only move one square at a time. When you land on a square, write the correct part of speech in the square and use it in an example sentence (spoken only). You can jump over squares which are already completed, but you cannot jump over walls or the other player's counter. You can move in any direction: forwards, backwards, left or right.

How to win

When neither player can add any more words, count how many words you have written in your pen colour. The player who has written the most correct words in the maze wins.

If...

- If you land on a square, but you don't know the part of speech, you miss a turn.
- If the other player makes a mistake, wait until it's your turn. Correct their mistake and you get two moves yourself!
- If the other player is in your way, you must go back. You cannot jump over another player.
- If you disagree about the correct answer or an example sentence, ask your teacher!

Word Formation Maze — Game board

VERB	NOUN	ADJECTIVE
e.g. satisfy		satisfactory
	decision	
amaze		
		competitive
	reception	
enable		
		observant
	sadness	
		forgivable
bore		
	communication	
		believable
succeed		
		imaginary
differ		e.g. different

Player A start here (top left) — Player B start here (bottom right)

Word Formation Maze — Answer Key

Verb	Noun	Adjective
satisfy	satisfaction	satisfactory
decide	decision	decisive
amaze	amazement	amazing
compete	competition	competitive
receive	reception	receptive
enable	ability	able
observe	observation	observant
sadden	sadness	sad

Verb	Noun	Adjective
forgive	forgiveness	forgivable
bore	boredom	boring / bored
communicate	communication	communicative
believe	belief	believable
succeed	success	successful
imagine	imagination	imaginary
differ	difference	different

© Delta Publishing 2014 — SPEAKING GAMES by Jason Anderson — Section 1: Board Games

Sport Busters

Time	15–30 minutes
Interaction	Pairs or small groups
Level	B1 (Intermediate) to C1 (Advanced)

Language areas practised

Sub-skills and Functions
- describing rules and conditions
- expressing obligation and prohibition

Grammar and Lexis
- modal verbs of obligation and prohibition
- sports

Preparation
Photocopy the **Rules of the game** and the **Game board** (one of each per 2 teams or pair of learners). At higher levels, learners can play individually against each other. At lower levels, teams of two or three are easier. Players need one dice per group. Take a few red and blue pens or pencils to class for any learners that don't have them.

How to win
Teams must link up their two sides of the board with their colour to win.

Notes
The Game board is based on the popular UK game show called *'Blockbusters'*. In the version here, there are no buzzers; teams take turns to nominate sports and win hexagons.

Variations
- **More Practice** – Learners mark the hexagons they win using pencil during a game. If they finish early, they can rub out the pencil and play again.

Sport Busters

Rules of the game

Preparation
Play in pairs or small teams of 2-3 players. You need a **Game board** and a dice. You also need two colours of pens or pencils (red and blue if possible). Decide who is 'The Reds' and who is 'The Blues'.

How to play
Roll the dice to see who goes first. The first team chooses any hexagon on the board and reads out the name of the sport. Then they roll the dice and answer the question on the Game board corresponding to the number on the dice for their sport. If they can answer the question correctly, they win the hexagon and colour it in. The next team then plays.

For example
The Reds go first, choose the hexagon *'football'* and roll a '3'. They now have to describe something the players aren't allowed to do, for example: *'The players can't touch the ball with their hands, except the goalkeeper.'* The Reds win the hexagon and colour it in red.

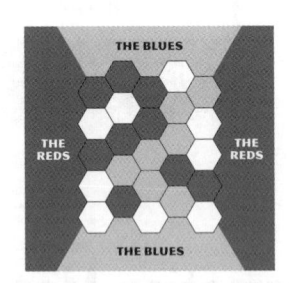

In this example, the blues win.

How to win
The first team to link their two sides of the board with their colour wins the game. This must be a continuous line of their colour. See the example above.

If...
- If a team isn't able to answer the question, they can't colour in the hexagon.
- If you disagree about the answer to a question, ask your teacher to play … as referee!

SPEAKING GAMES by Jason Anderson © Delta Publishing 2014

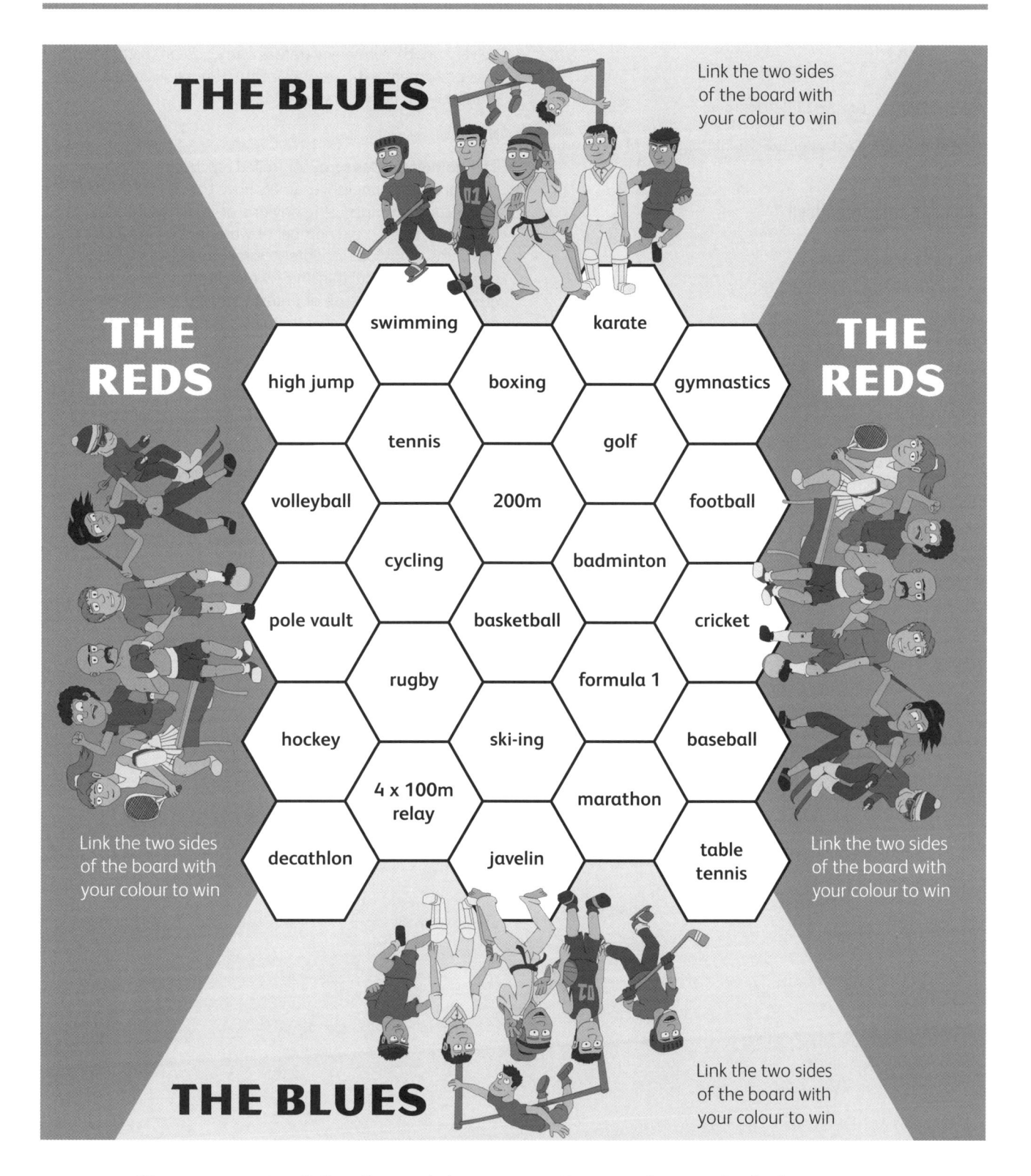

Sport Busters

Game board

THE BLUES

Link the two sides of the board with your colour to win

THE REDS

	swimming	karate
high jump	boxing	gymnastics
	tennis	golf
volleyball	200m	football
	cycling	badminton
pole vault	basketball	cricket
	rugby	formula 1
hockey	ski-ing	baseball
	4 x 100m relay	marathon
decathlon	javelin	table tennis

THE REDS

Link the two sides of the board with your colour to win

THE BLUES

Link the two sides of the board with your colour to win

Choose a sport, roll the dice and then answer the question to win the hexagon:

- ⚀ Where do you do this sport?
- ⚁ What equipment do you need to do this sport?
- ⚂ What aren't the players or participants allowed to do?
- ⚃ What do the players or participants have to do to win?
- ⚄ What happens if the players or participants break the rules?
- ⚅ Name a famous person in this sport.

© Delta Publishing 2014 SPEAKING GAMES by Jason Anderson

Phrasal Verb Addiction

Time	15–30 minutes
Interaction	Groups of 3–4 learners
Level	B2 (Upper Intermediate) to C1 (Advanced)

Language areas practised

Sub-skills and Functions

- responding quickly to questions

Grammar and Lexis

- phrasal verbs

Preparation

Photocopy the **Rules of the game**, the **Game board** and the **Phrasal Verb question cards** from page 118 of the Resource bank (one of each per group). Cut up the questions cards as indicated. With lower level classes, make sure they know the following phrasal verbs before you start: *go off* (stop liking), *go up* (increase – price), *turn out* (conclude: it turned out to be very good), *turn away* (refuse entry), *go on* (continue), *take on* (accept extra responsibility). If possible, teach these phrasal verbs earlier in the lesson.

Notes

This game provides semi-controlled practice of 20 common phrasal verbs in English. Learners have to respond quickly to question prompts using any one of 20 phrasal verbs. Obviously, there are a number of ways that a player can use the phrasal verb appropriately. Some are fairly easy, others require some lateral thinking – which tends to lead to lots of guesses, and lots of use of phrasal verbs! If they fail to guess any phrasal verbs, go over them as a class at the end.

Variations

- **Lower Levels** – If no-one guesses the correct answer, the player asking the question can give them a hint by telling them the verb or the particle.

- **Mingle Activity** – Forget the Game board. Write the four verbs and five particles on the board in random locations. Give each learner a question. They stand, mingle and award each other a point if they get the answer.

SPEAKING GAMES by Jason Anderson © Delta Publishing 2014

Phrasal Verb Addiction

Rules of the game

Preparation
Play in groups of 3-4. Each group needs a **Game board** and a set of **Phrasal Verb question cards**. Put the Question cards face down in a pile next to the board.

How to play
Take turns to pick up a Question card and read out the question (keeping the phrasal verb secret). The other players must try to answer the question using one of the phrasal verbs from the Game board. The first player to answer the question using the phrasal verb on the Question card wins the square on the board. She should write her name on the square. For example, Player A takes the following card:

Aren't you hot, sitting in your coat?	take off

If one of the other players says: *'Yes, I think I'll take it off.'* or something similar, she wins the square.

How to win
When all the squares have been won, or all the phrasal verb cards have been used, count how many squares each player has won. The player who has won the most squares is the winner.

If...
- If you only say the phrasal verb on the card, you don't win the square. You must use the phrasal verb in a full sentence in order to win.
- If no player is able to use the phrasal verb on the Question card, put the card at the bottom of the pile.
- If you use a different phrasal verb from the board to answer the question, you don't win the square, even if your answer is logical.

Phrasal Verb Addiction

Game board

	get	take	go	turn	
off	get off	take off	go off	turn off	off
up	get up	take up	go up	turn up	up
out	get out	take out	go out	turn out	out
on	get on	take on	go on	turn on	on
away	get away	take away	go away	turn away	away
	get	take	go	turn	

© Delta Publishing 2014 — SPEAKING GAMES by Jason Anderson

Personality Connections

Time	20–30 minutes
Interaction	Groups of 2–4 learners
Level	B1 (Intermediate) to C1 (Advanced)

Language areas practised

Sub-skills and Functions

- describing characteristics and personality

Grammar and Lexis

- adjectives to describe personality

Preparation

Photocopy the **Rules of the game**, the **Game board** and the **Personality question cards** on page 34 (one of each per group). Cut up the Question cards as indicated. Lower level classes may prefer to play in teams of two. Check the meaning and pronunciation of any unfamiliar adjectives before they begin playing.

Notes

This game is loosely based on *Connect Four*, a popular puzzle game. The rules have been modified as follows: learners can start anywhere on the board and can play either in pairs or groups of up to four - which leads to more interesting tactics.

Variations

- **Simpler** – Players just define the adjectives to win the square.

Personality Connections — Rules of the game

Preparation

Play in groups of 2-4. Each group needs a **Game board** and a set of **Personality question cards**. Put the question cards in a pile face down. Each player should choose a symbol from the following four choices: ✗ ○ □ ♥

How to play

Take turns to choose a square and take the top Question card from the pile. You then answer the question about the personality adjective in the chosen square. For example: *'What jobs is a punctual person good at?'* If you are able to answer the question, you win the square and write your symbol on it. When the Question cards have all been used, shuffle them and put them back in a pile.

How to win

The aim of the game is to get four of your symbols in a straight line – horizontally, diagonally or vertically. The first player to do this is the winner. If there is a draw at the end, the player with the highest number of three symbols in a row becomes the winner.

If...

- If you aren't able to answer a question, you are allowed to take a second question card. If you can't answer this question, you lose your turn.
- If you are not sure if an answer is correct, ask your teacher.

Personality Connections — Game board

outgoing	funny	faithful	honest	sensible	energetic	naïve
serious	wise	ambitious	romantic	helpful	caring	crafty
friendly	bossy	organised	calm	fun	gentle	nervous
easy-going	sociable	generous	sensitive	punctual	mean	unreliable
quiet	clever	shy	confident	selfish	polite	aggressive

Personality Connections

Personality question cards

What jobs is a _____ person good at?	Are you _____? Give reasons for your answer.	Describe somebody you know who is _____. Do you like him/her?
Is this a positive or a negative characteristic? Or does it depend? Explain your answer.	Which nationality do you associate with being _____? Why?	How would you translate this adjective into your language?
Is this characteristic more common in men or women? Give reasons for your answer.	What does _____ mean?	What is the opposite of _____?
Who in this class is _____? Why do you think this?	Choose a famous person who is _____. How do you know s/he is _____?	Pretend you are _____.
Can this adjective only be used to describe people? If not, how else can it be used.	How many syllables does this adjective have? Where does the stress fall?	Think of an animal that is _____. Give reasons for your choice.

Section 1: Board Games

SPEAKING GAMES by Jason Anderson © Delta Publishing 2014

Description Bingo

Time	20–35 minutes
Interaction	Groups of 4–8 learners
Level	B1 (Intermediate) to B2 (Upper Intermediate)

Language areas practised

Sub-skills and Functions
- describing appearance
- asking *yes / no* questions

Grammar and Lexis
- adjective order
- *have got / have*
- features of the face

Preparation
Photocopy the **Rules of the game** (two or three per group), the **Face cards** (one set per group) and the **Bingo cards** (one per player). Cut up the Face cards and Bingo cards as indicated. Put each set of Face cards into a bag.

Before the learners begin, point out that the faces are very similar. Therefore they should describe and listen carefully, asking questions to check if necessary. Monitor carefully to make sure they understand the rules.

Notes
This is a variation of the classic bingo numbers game that requires both careful description and careful listening. It is played in groups to maximise speaking practice.

Variations
- **Whole Class Variation** – Players play as a whole class with individuals coming to the front to take a Face card from the bag and describing it.
- **Bingo Mingle** – Copy the Bingo cards only. Distribute to players who stand and mingle. When they meet another player one of the pair describes one of their six faces. If the other player has the same face, both can cross it off. They should also write the name of the other player next to the face (so *'Bingo!'* claims can be checked afterwards). The other player then describes one of their faces. After one description each, they change partners. The first learner to cross off all their faces says: *'Bingo!'*

Description Bingo   Rules of the game

Preparation
Play in groups of 4-8. Each group needs a bag of **Face cards** and each player needs a **Bingo card**.

How to play
Take turns to pick a Face card from the bag and describe it to the other players. Don't show the picture. The other players can ask you questions. For example: *'Has he got a moustache?' 'Is his hair curly?'* etc. Any player (including you) who thinks they have this face on their Bingo card can cross it off. Remember that the face that is being described may not be on your card. You then place the Face card face down on the desk, so no-one can see it. Don't put it back in the bag. Play continues in this way until someone says: *'Bingo!'*.

How to win
The first player to cross off all six faces on their Bingo card says: *'Bingo!'*. Check the Face cards on the table without letting the other players see. If you can find your six faces, you have won. If not, you have made a mistake – so keep playing!

© Delta Publishing 2014   SPEAKING GAMES by Jason Anderson

Description Bingo — Face cards

Section 1: Board Games

SPEAKING GAMES by Jason Anderson © Delta Publishing 2014

Description Bingo

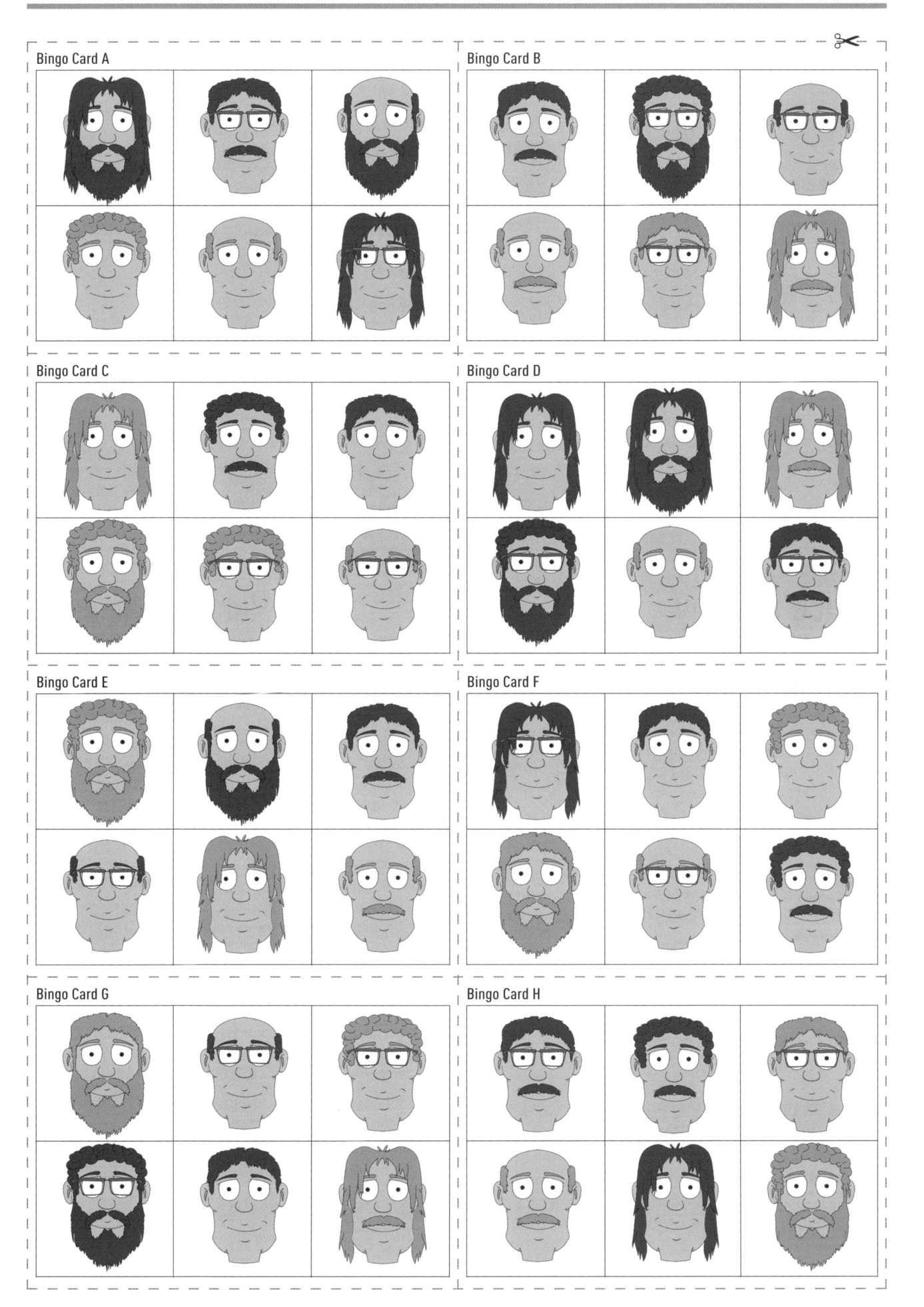

Bingo cards

Bingo Card A

Bingo Card B

Bingo Card C

Bingo Card D

Bingo Card E

Bingo Card F

Bingo Card G

Bingo Card H

Section 1: Board Games

© Delta Publishing 2014

SPEAKING GAMES by Jason Anderson

Advice Rummy

Time	20–30 minutes
Interaction	Groups of 3–5 learners
Level	B1 (Intermediate) to B2 (Upper Intermediate)

Language areas practised

Sub-skills and Functions

- giving advice
- thinking of creative solutions to problems

Grammar and Lexis

- *should, could, ought to*, etc. for giving advice

Preparation

Photocopy the **Rules of the game** and both sets of cards (one copy of each per group). Cut up the cards as indicated.

You may wish to show learners how to play the card game with a demonstration: get all the learners to stand around one group while you play one round with them.

Notes

Several cards could potentially provide advice for each problem if learners think creatively. There are no wrong answers as long as the learners in a group agree that the advice is useful. If your learners are particularly competitive, they may find it more difficult to win cards, but the disputes will provide plenty of speaking practice and use of the advice structures!

Variations

- **More Personalisation** – Learners each add two or three problems of their own to the pile of Problem cards before they begin playing. You'll need some extra slips of paper for this.

Advice Rummy

Rules of the game

Preparation

Play in groups of 3-5. Your teacher will give you two sets of cards. Put the big cards in a pile, face down on your desk: these are the **Problem cards**. Put the small cards in a different pile next to them: these are the **Advice cards**. Each player should take two Advice cards. Players can look at their Advice cards.

How to play

Player A takes the top Problem card and reads out the problem. Player B tries to think of some advice using one of her Advice cards. For example, Player A reads the card on the left and Player B has the card on the right.

| I want a new mobile phone but I don't have much money. | birthday |

Player B could say:

'You should ask for a new one for your birthday.'

If Player A agrees that this is good advice, Player B wins the Problem card and keeps it with the Advice card. He can't use the advice card again. If he has only one Advice card left, he should take another from the pile. If Player B can't give any good advice using his cards, he must pick up another Advice card (he can't use this card until the next round). Player C can now try to give advice to Player A. If she can't, she must also pick up an Advice card. The round continues in this way. Player B reads out the Problem card to start the next round.

How to win

The game finishes when all the Problem cards are won. Each player should count their Problem cards and Advice cards. You score three points for every problem card you have, but you lose one point for every Advice card you have. The player with the most points wins!

If...

- If nobody can give you advice for your problem, you can use one of your Advice cards to give yourself advice: *'I ought to wait until my birthday.'* If others agree it's good advice, you win the Problem card!

- If nobody can give any useful advice for a problem, put the card at the bottom of the pile.

- If there are no more Advice cards to take, all the players must try to finish the game using the Advice cards they have in their hand.

Advice Rummy — Problem cards

I'm trying to learn to play the guitar but it's too difficult.	I want to lose weight.	My watch keeps stopping.
I keep forgetting all the new words I learn in class.	I really like someone, but I don't know how to ask them out.	I'm tired of my job.
I keep waking up with headaches.	I'm spending too much money on public transport.	I can't get to sleep at night.
I find it difficult to get up in the morning.	My skin is too dry.	I'm tired of my appearance.

Advice Rummy — Advice cards

lessons	junk food	some new batteries	a dog	a boring book	university
a vocabulary notebook	swimming	a holiday	coffee	your teacher	cheese
drink water	a bicycle	the piano	a gym	Facebook	birthday
an alarm clock	glasses	a good hairdresser	shoes	cold showers	moisturiser

Section 2: Card Games

© Delta Publishing 2014   SPEAKING GAMES by Jason Anderson

Grammar Gym

Time	10–15 minutes
Interaction	Pairs
Level	B1 (Intermediate) to B2 (Upper Intermediate)

Language areas practised

Sub-skills and Functions

- conjugating verbs accurately at speed

Grammar and Lexis

- all tenses / aspects that your learners already know

Preparation

Photocopy the **Grammar Gym cards** and the **Rules of the game** (one copy of each per pair). Cut up the cards as indicated. There are 12 tenses / aspects provided. If there are any tenses that your learners haven't studied, you can remove them.

Notes

Grammar Gym provides a structural drill in the form of a game. Regular use (15 minutes once or twice a week) can significantly improve learners' speed and accuracy in conjugating verbs. It may take some time to cut up the sets, but they can be reused regularly over a period of several months or years, especially if laminated.

Variations

- **Less Cutting Up Variation** – Learners play in groups of 3-4 with each learner taking control of 1-2 piles of cards.

Grammar Gym

Preparation

Play in pairs. Your teacher will give you a set of **Grammar Gym cards**. These consist of four groups: pronouns (*you, she*, etc.), sentence forms (positive, negative or question), verb tenses (present simple, past simple, etc.) and verb phrases (*go home, watch TV,* etc.) . Each player should have sets of cards for two different groups and place them in two separate piles, face down. Each pair also needs a pen and paper to keep score.

How to play

Both players turn over their top cards from both their piles at the same time and put them face up on the table. Look at the information on the four cards and try to say the sentence as quickly as you can. For example, you turn over:

| she | NEGATIVE | **past simple** | listen to music |

Rules of the game

The sentence is: *'She didn't listen to music.'* The first player to say this sentence wins one point. When you finish your cards, shuffle and start again. Keep playing to practise getting your tenses right!

How to win

The player with the highest score wins.

If...

- If you say an incorrect sentence, no point is scored and the other player can try to make the sentence.
- If you both say the correct sentence simultaneously, you both win a point.
- If you both make a mistake, you can try again.

Grammar Gym — Cards

I	you	we
he	she	they
POSITIVE	NEGATIVE	QUESTION
POSITIVE	NEGATIVE	QUESTION
present simple	**present continuous**	**past simple**
past continuous	**future simple (will)**	**future continuous**
going to future	**present perfect simple**	**present perfect continuous**
past simple	**past perfect continuous**	**future perfect simple**
read a magazine	*use the Internet*	*have dinner*
check the news	*send an email*	*go home*
watch TV	*listen to music*	*do the shopping*

Section 2: Card Games

Say the Right Thing

Time	15–30 minutes
Interaction	Whole class
Level	B1 (Intermediate) to C1 (Advanced)

Language areas practised

Sub-skills and Functions
- responding appropriately to good / bad news
- using intonation and body language to convey meaning

Grammar and Lexis
- *So do I. / Me too.*
- spoken attention signals

Preparation
Photocopy the **Rules of the game** (one copy per pair) and the **Say the Right Thing cards** on pages 43 and 44 (one card per learner). If you have more than 12 learners in your class, give some cards out twice. If you have over 15 learners, create two groups. At lower levels begin with a few examples, letting the learners choose from the responses in the **Useful Expressions** box shown in the Rules of the game. Use the following (or similar comments) as examples and encourage appropriate responses after each one:

Your shoes are lovely!
My parrot just died.
Somebody smells terrible in here.
I've just got engaged.

Notes
Make sure learners understand that their responses to Starters should be improvised and do not have to come from their own card.

Variations
- **Say the Wrong Thing!** – The learners try to score the lowest points possible by guessing the '–1 point' option. This can be good fun after they've practised saying the right thing!

Say the Right Thing — Rules of the game

Preparation
Play as a whole class. Your teacher will give you a **Say the Right Thing card**. Remember your 'Starter'. You will use this to start conversations with other learners. You should also read the 'Responses', but keep them secret and don't show them to anyone else. You'll also need a pen to keep score.

How to play
Everybody stands and talks to other learners in pairs. When you meet another learner, one of you should say your 'starter'. The other should try to respond appropriately. If he uses any of the statements under 'Responses', give him the points. If he doesn't, say: *'Try again'* and give him one more go. Then the other learner should start a conversation with their 'starter'. When the two exchanges are complete, change partners.

How to win
Note down any points you score on your own card. The player with the highest score at the end of the game wins.

If…
- If somebody responds with a comment very similar to one you have under 'Responses', you can give them the points. It doesn't have to be identical.
- If somebody gives the right response, but not the right body language or intonation, give them half the points.
- In a large class you might hear the same 'Starter'. This is an opportunity to get it right the second time!

Example Expressions

Congratulations!   Me too!   Oh no!
Actually,…   I beg your pardon!
That's a shame.   Well done!   Oh dear.
Good for you!   That's really kind of you.
Oh you poor thing!   Do you really think so?

Say the Right Thing — Cards

Your starter is...
'I hate boring films.'
Responses:

3 points	So do I! Me too! Especially…
2 points	Really? Why?
1 point	Do you? I don't. Doesn't everybody?
-1 point	So? So what? Who cares?

Your Score Card

Your starter is...
'I love your hairstyle. It really suits you.'
Responses:

3 points	Oh, thank you. That's really kind of you.
2 points	Thanks. Do you think so?
1 point	I know. Everyone says so.
-1 point	Yours doesn't. It's better than yours.

Your Score Card

Your starter is...
'I forgot your birthday last week. I'm so sorry!'
Responses:

3 points	I wouldn't worry about it! So did I! That's OK. I forgot yours too.
2 points	That's fine. Actually, so did…
1 point	No problem. What birthday?
-1 point	I thought you were my friend! Sorry! I'll never forgive you.

Your Score Card

Your starter is...
'My boy/girlfriend/wife/husband has just left me for my best friend!'
Responses:

3 points	Oh you poor thing! Is there anything I can do for you?
2 points	Oh no! There's plenty more fish in the sea! I didn't like him anyway.
1 point	Cheer up! Don't worry. That's a shame.
-1 point	Who cares? Pull yourself together.

Your Score Card

Your starter is...
'I've just passed my driving test!'
Responses:

3 points	Congratulations! That's (wonderful/fantastic) news!
2 points	Well done! Was it your first (attempt / time)?
1 point	Let's celebrate…
-1 point	So what? I passed years ago.

Your Score Card

Your starter is...
'I've just given up smoking.'
Responses:

3 points	Good for you! Let me know if…
2 points	Well done. Good luck with it.
1 point	Congratulations.
-1 point	Shame! It suited you.

Your Score Card

© Delta Publishing 2014   SPEAKING GAMES by Jason Anderson

Section 2: Card Games

Say the Right Thing — Cards

Section 2: Card Games

Your starter is…	Your Score Card
'Has anyone ever told you that you're very annoying?'	
Responses:	
3 points — I beg your pardon! How dare you!	
2 points — Actually, so are you.	
1 point — No. Never.	
-1 point — Yes. All the time. I know.	

Your starter is…	Your Score Card
'I've lost my pen again!'	
Responses:	
3 points — That's a shame. Have you looked in…?	
2 points — Oh dear. What does it look like?	
1 point — Have you? What a pity.	
-1 point — Typical! It's in your hand, dummy. I know. I stole it.	

Your starter is…	Your Score Card
'I think I've broken your phone.'	
Responses:	
3 points — You're joking. Oh no!	
2 points — What happened? Let me see.	
1 point — What?! How did you do it?	
-1 point — You idiot! You stupid fool! Damn you!	

Your starter is…	Your Score Card
'You know – that colour doesn't really suit you.'	
Responses:	
3 points — Do you really think so? What colour does suit me?	
2 points — Oh, really? Thanks for letting me know.	
1 point — Which one? Yes it does.	
-1 point — Get lost! Mind your own business!	

Your starter is…	Your Score Card
'I'm not feeling very well. I think I'm going to be sick.'	
Responses:	
3 points — Come and sit down. Can I get you anything?	
2 points — Oh dear. Can I do anything? Let me get you some water.	
1 point — Oh no! Not here! Go to the bathroom/toilet.	
-1 point — Get away from me. Don't be sick on me!	

Your starter is…	Your Score Card
'I'm feeling much better after my cold last week.'	
Responses:	
3 points — Good for you. You look much better.	
2 points — That's good to hear. You were really under the weather.	
1 point — Good. I hope you didn't give it to me.	
-1 point — Good. You can stop moaning now. You're always talking about yourself.	

'Both' & 'Neither' Snap

Time	10–20 minutes
Interaction	Groups of 3–4 players
Level	B1 (Intermediate) to C1 (Advanced)

Language areas practised

Sub-skills and Functions
- thinking creatively under time pressure
- drawing comparisons
- challenging the validity of a statement

Grammar and Lexis
- *both* and *neither*
- *have to* for obligation
- occupations

Preparation
Photocopy the **Rules of the game** (one copy per group) and the **Job cards** from page 115 of the Resource bank (one set per group). Cut up the Job cards as indicated. With lower level classes, put a few useful verb phrases on the board before beginning the game and discuss which jobs match each one. For example:

…wear a uniform …work outdoors
….work with tools …earn a lot of money

Notes
Learners can challenge a response (see Rules of the game) This often generates richer interaction between learners than the *both/neither* sentences themselves, especially in competitive classes! If groups finish quickly, they can shuffle the cards and play again.

Variations
- **Pairwork Variation** – Learners play in pairs with both players taking half the cards and turning over one card at the same time.
- **Vocab Variation** – Learners play with cards of a different lexical set. For example, if the learners have recently studied food and cooking, images of different ingredients could be used.
- **Describing Appearance** – Learners describe the images rather than the jobs (e.g. 'Both are wearing hats.').

'Both' & 'Neither' Snap — Rules of the game

Preparation
Play in groups of 3-4. Your teacher will give you a set of **Job cards**, all of which have images of people doing different jobs on them. Look through them quickly to identify the jobs, then shuffle the cards. Divide the cards into two piles of equal size and place them next to each other on the table, face down.

How to play
One player turns over the top two Job cards at the same time and places them together. The first player to say a sentence that links the two jobs using *both* or *neither* wins both cards. For example, if the cards are waitress and policeman, you could say: *'both have to wear uniforms'*, or: *'neither a waitress nor a policeman works with animals'*. The winner keeps both the cards. A different player turns over the next two cards.

How to win
The player with the most cards at the end of the game wins!

If…
- If nobody can think of a *both* or *neither* sentence, turn over another from either pile and place it next to the other two. You can compare it with either of the other two cards to win all three cards.
- If you think another player's sentence isn't true, you can challenge it. For example: *'A policeman sometimes works with animals if, for example, they are blocking the road.'* If the others agree with your challenge and you can provide a different true sentence with *both* or *neither*, you win the cards.

Just a Minute!

Time	20–30 minutes
Interaction	Groups of 3–5 players
Level	B1 (Intermediate) to C1 (Advanced)

Language areas practised

Sub-skills and Functions

- monitoring accuracy while speaking fluently
- peer-correcting errors

Grammar and Lexis

- spoken fillers (*well*, *erm*, *right*, etc.)
- spoken hedging expressions (*I suppose…*, *And also…*, etc.)

Preparation

Photocopy the **Rules of the game** and the **Topic cards** from pages 123–124 of the Resource bank (one of each per group). Choose between the 'easy' Topic cards for lower levels, and the 'challenging' Topic cards for higher levels. Cut up the cards as indicated. Learners will also need one-minute timers (e.g. on mobile phones). The easiest way to check understanding of the rules is to choose a topic and talk for a minute as an example. You can encourage the learners to challenge by pausing and making mistakes.

Notes

This game is based on a popular BBC radio game show of the same name. The key difference is how players challenge each other. The two challenges are *'Error!'* and *'Pause!'*, meaning that learners are trying to focus on both accuracy and fluency at the same time: learners monitor their own production when they are speaking and each other's production when they are listening. Be ready to mediate disputed challenges!

Variations

- Advanced learners may want to play the game as it's played on the radio, where challenges are made for hesitation (pausing), deviation (drifting off topic) and repetition (when they repeat an idea or a topic word). Be aware that this is quite a challenge even for native speakers!
- You could play the game using the **Opinion cards** in the Resource bank (page 116) instead of the Topic cards.

Just a Minute! — Rules of the game

Preparation

Play in groups of 3-5. Your teacher will give you a set of **Topic cards**. Put them in a pile face down. You also need a timer (e.g. mobile phone) to count from one minute down to zero.

How to play

Take turns to start. The first speaker takes the top Topic card and shows it to the group. She must speak on that topic for one minute. The other players start the timer. The speaker must not pause for over three seconds or make any errors during this time. Other players can challenge the speaker by saying: *'Stop!'* if they think she has either paused or made an error. When a player challenges the speaker, pause the timer (see *If…* notes).

How to score and win

The player who is speaking at the end of one minute wins one point. Players score one point for each successful challenge. The player who has the most points at the end of the game wins.

If…

- If you think the speaker has paused for more than three seconds, you can challenge him by saying: *'Pause!'* If the challenge is accepted, you win one point. You now take over the topic and must continue talking on the same topic for the time remaining on the timer (e.g. 20 seconds).
- If you think the speaker has made an error (grammar, pronunciation, etc.), you can challenge her by saying: *'Error!'* If the challenge is accepted, you win one point. You then take over as explained above.
- If a challenge (pause or error) is not accepted, the challenger loses one point and the original speaker continues for the remaining time.

Dragons' Lair

Time	40–60 minutes
Interaction	Groups of three teams (1-3 players per team)
Level	B2 (Upper Intermediate) to C1 (Advanced)

Language areas practised

Sub-skills and Functions

- pitching an original business idea
- responding to probing questions

Grammar and Lexis

- 1st conditional structures
- 2nd conditional structures
- business and finance

Preparation

Photocopy the **Rules of the game** and the **Bright Idea card** (one of each per team). Also copy the **What if…? cards** on page 49 (one set per group) and cut up as indicated. Numbers are quite flexible for this game: although each group requires three teams, each team could have one, two or three players and the number of players in each team doesn't have to be the same. Lower level classes will benefit from larger teams; higher level/business English learners will be able to play alone. When you give out the What if…? cards, make sure that the top two cards aren't 'You Choose the Question'. This will give them time to get into the game before they have to think of their own questions.

Notes

This game is based loosely on the *Dragons' Den* television show and aims to provide learners with practice choosing between 1st and 2nd conditional structures. The questioner may choose either conditional structure depending on whether they want to indicate high probability (1st conditional) or low probability (2nd conditional). The respondent may want to change the conditional to reduce or increase the implied probability as might happen in real life. For example:

'What will you do if you make a loss in your 1st year?'

'If we made a loss, first we would…' etc.

You may want to explain this or provide an example before they start. Alternatively, if you just want to practise either 1st or 2nd conditional, all the cards lend themselves to both.

Variations

- **TV Show Variation** – Turn it into a role play with several stages. First the teams prepare their ideas. Then they present to the other teams who play the role of the Dragons (the investors). The What if…? cards can be used by the teams to provide ideas for questions after each presentation. At the end, each team decides which of the other teams they'd invest in if they were a tycoon. The team that attracts the most investors wins.

Section 2: Card Games

Dragons' Lair

Rules of the game

Preparation
Play in groups of three teams. Each team should have 1-3 members. Complete a **Bright Idea card** in your team with details of your business idea.

Each group will also need a set of **What if…? cards**. Put them in a pile, face down in the middle of the table.

How to play
Each team begins by briefly presenting their business idea to the other teams.

After this, Team A should take the first What if…? card and ask a question using 1st or 2nd conditional. The other teams (B and C) must try to answer the question about their own business idea. Team A then decides which team (B or C) gave the best answer and invests $10,000 in this team by giving them the card. Team B takes the next What if…? card and asks the question to teams C and A. The game continues like this until all the What if…? cards have been used.

How to win
Any team that gets the initial investment sum that they wrote on their Bright Idea card wins!

If…
- If you pick up a card that looks like this,

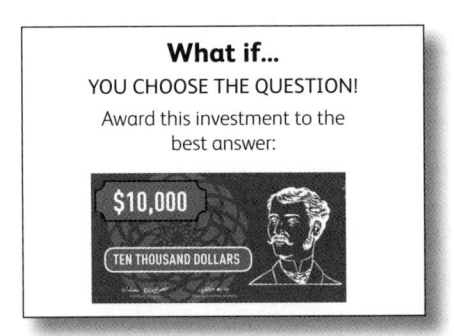

> **What if…**
> YOU CHOOSE THE QUESTION!
> Award this investment to the best answer:
>
> **$10,000**
> TEN THOUSAND DOLLARS

you should think of your own What if…? question to ask the other two teams about their business ideas. You may choose the same question for the two teams, or different questions that relate to their individual business ideas. As with other questions, you choose who to invest in.

Our Bright Idea!

Think of an original idea to make money. It might be a business idea, an invention or an app. You will need to present your idea to the other teams and then answer questions about your business plan. Complete the following details:

Name:

Brief synopsis of idea:

Initial investment needed (up to $70,000 US dollars):

SPEAKING GAMES by Jason Anderson © Delta Publishing 2014

Dragons' Lair

What if...? cards

What if...
1st year profits (be) lower than expected?
Award this investment to the best answer:

What if...
somebody (try) to steal your idea?
Award this investment to the best answer:

What if...
somebody (offer) you a better job?
Award this investment to the best answer:

What if...
a key investor (withdraw) for personal reasons?
Award this investment to the best answer:

What if...
you (have to) take time off due to stress/exhaustion?
Award this investment to the best answer:

What if...
you (find) a serious design fault in the product?
Award this investment to the best answer:

What if...
there (be) negative feedback in the press?
Award this investment to the best answer:

What if...
somebody (accuse) you of stealing their idea?
Award this investment to the best answer:

What if...
you (make) a million dollars in your first year?
Award this investment to the best answer:

What if...
you (not agree) with your investor?
Award this investment to the best answer:

What if...
you (find) that you (be) only using 50% of your advertising budget?
Award this investment to the best answer:

What if...
Google (want) to take over your company?
Award this investment to the best answer:

What if...
YOU CHOOSE THE QUESTION!
Award this investment to the best answer:

What if...
YOU CHOOSE THE QUESTION!
Award this investment to the best answer:

What if...
YOU CHOOSE THE QUESTION!
Award this investment to the best answer:

What if...
YOU CHOOSE THE QUESTION!
Award this investment to the best answer:

What if...
YOU CHOOSE THE QUESTION!
Award this investment to the best answer:

What if...
YOU CHOOSE THE QUESTION!
Award this investment to the best answer:

Section 2: Card Games

© Delta Publishing 2014

SPEAKING GAMES by Jason Anderson

Original Opinions

Time	20–40 minutes
Interaction	Groups of 3–5 players
Level	B1 (Intermediate) to C1 (Advanced)

Language areas practised

Sub-skills and Functions

- expressing opinions
- agreeing and disagreeing
- describing conditions

Grammar and Lexis

- zero conditional structures
- expressions for giving opinions

Preparation

Photocopy the **Rules of the game** and the **Opinion cards** from page 116 of the Resource bank (one of each per group). Remove any Opinion cards that you feel may be unsuitable for your learners. Also copy one set of the three **Agreement cards** (on the next page) per learner. Cut up each set of cards as indicated. With lower level classes, do an example round with one group while the others watch.

Notes

This game encourages learners to give original opinions compared to their classmates. It works best with learners who know each other well and are able to predict each other's opinions. This leads to them choosing an opinion that they think is original in order to score more points. Tactical bluffing and double bluffing are common. The 'it depends' card often leads to the learners describing conditions, i.e. what it depends on.

Variations

- Learners don't choose their agreement card at the start. They wait for their turn and choose which card to play based on what the previous players have chosen. This version relies less on luck, but requires very quick thinking and only works with groups of four or more.

Original Opinions — Rules of the game

Preparation

Play in groups of 3-5. Each player needs a set of three **Agreement cards**: 'agree', 'disagree' and 'it depends'. Each group also needs a set of **Opinion cards**. Place these in a pile, face down.

How to play

Player A should turn over the top Opinion card. Every player should silently read the card and decide whether they agree or disagree with the opinion, or think that 'it depends'. Without letting the other players see, each player then chooses the Agreement card that reflects their opinion and places it face down on the table in front of them, keeping it secret. When everybody has done this, Player A shows her card and expresses her opinion, providing a reason. Player B then does the same, then Player C, etc. Score points for that round after all the players have expressed their opinions. Player B starts the next round.

How to score

You score points for having original opinions in this game. After each round, look at the cards everybody has played. If nobody else has played the same card as you, you score three points. If only one player has played the same card as you, you score two points. If two players have played the same card as you, you score one point. If three or more players have played the same card, you score zero points.

How to win

The player with the highest score at the end of the game wins.

If...

- If you like, you can express opinions that aren't your real opinion, as long as you provide a logical reason for the opinion.
- If you aren't able to provide a logical reason for your opinion, you are disqualified from that round and can't score any points.

Original Opinions — Game board

agree	disagree	it depends
agree	disagree	it depends
agree	disagree	it depends
agree	disagree	it depends
agree	disagree	it depends
agree	disagree	it depends
agree	disagree	it depends
agree	disagree	it depends

The Thing about Cleft Sentences...

Time	20–30 minutes
Interaction	Groups of 3–4 players
Level	B2 (Upper Intermediate) to C1 (Advanced)

Language areas practised

Sub-skills and Functions
- commenting on a topic / issue
- expressing opinions
- providing supporting arguments
- adding emphasis

Grammar and Lexis
- cleft sentences
- *it* as a preparatory subject
- complex sentences

Preparation

Photocopy the **Rules of the game**, the **Topic cards** and the **Phrase cards** (one of each per group). Cut up the cards as indicated. With lower level classes, take them through a few examples before they play. With higher level classes, remind them that other options may be possible (e.g. *It's so difficult if ...* in the example), and that they are free to use them if they wish.

Notes

This game provides practice using both cleft sentences (e.g. *'What I like about Facebook is it's so easy to stay in touch with friends.'*) and preparatory *'It'* structures (e.g. *'It's surprising how the Internet has become so important in our lives.'*) Both are important for evaluating or commenting on a topic in informal (especially spoken) English. Note that some *'It'* clauses can have several possible completions:

It's so difficult   when children become teenagers.
　　　　　　　　　 to find nutritious food nowadays.
　　　　　　　　　 avoiding pollution in a big city.

You may need to clarify any difficult ones at the end of the activity.

Variations

- **More Topics** – Use the Topic cards from the Resource bank (pages 123–124) for a greater variety of topics.
- **Pairwork** – Learners play in pairs, taking turns to turn over a Topic card and a Phrase card at the same time and then formulate a sentence on the topic that starts with that phrase.

The Thing about Cleft Sentences...   Rules of the game

Preparation

Play in groups of 3-4. Each group needs a set of **Topic cards** and a set of **Phrase cards**. Put the Topic cards in a pile, face down in the middle of the table. Deal out three Phrase cards to each player and put the remaining Phrase cards in a pile face down next to the Topic cards. Players can look at their three Phrase cards.

How to play

Player A turns over the top Topic card for the others to see and tries to think of a comment on the topic using the phrase on one of his Phrase cards. He places the card on the table and picks up a new Phrase card from the pile on the table. Player B then tries to use one of her Phrase cards to comment on the same topic. The round finishes when all players have commented once on the topic. Clear the played cards to one side (you won't need them again). Player B starts the next round.

How to win

When all the Phrase cards in the pile on the table have been picked up, the game becomes a race to win! The first player to get rid of all his Phrase cards wins.

If...

- If you can't think of a sentence on the topic using one of your Phrase cards, you must still pick up a new Phrase card. Some players could have four or more Phrase cards as a result.
- If you think another player has used a Phrase card incorrectly or inappropriately, you can challenge him. The other players must decide if the challenge is valid. If it is, he must pick up a Phrase card without playing one. If you aren't sure about a challenge, ask your teacher.

The Thing about Cleft Sentences... Topic cards

pop music	Facebook	television	children
football	restaurants	credit cards	the Internet
Hollywood movies	shopping	fashion	the environment

The Thing about Cleft Sentences... Phrase cards

What I like about… is…	It's interesting [that / to / how / verb+ing]…	The reason why… is…	I think it's important to…
The problem with… is…	It's surprising [that / when / how]…	There are two reasons why…	I'm not sure that…
It's true that…	It's really fun [when / to / verb+ing]…	It's so difficult [when / to / verb+ing]…	What really annoys me about… is…
It's dangerous [when / to / verb+ing]…	It's really stupid [when / to / verb+ing]…	The good thing about… is…	It's so easy [to / verb+ing]…
What I don't understand about… is…	It's worth [verb+ing]…	It's good [that / when / to / how / [verb+ing]…	One problem I've always had with… is…
It's no good [verb+ing]…	It's not a good idea to…	One of the things I don't like about… is…	It's no use [verb+ing]…

© Delta Publishing 2014   SPEAKING GAMES by Jason Anderson

Section 2: Card Games

Pros and Cons Dice

Time	15–30 minutes
Interaction	Groups of 3–5 learners
Level	B1 (Intermediate) to C1 (Advanced)

Language areas practised

Sub-skills and Functions
- generating ideas quickly
- challenging an idea

Grammar and Lexis
- comparative structures

Preparation
Photocopy the **Rules of the game** and the **Pros and Cons cards** from page 119 of the Resource bank (one of each per group). Cut up the cards as indicated. You also need a dice for each group.

Notes
The opportunity to 'steal points' means that the players have to listen to each other carefully. The opportunity to question the validity of an advantage/disadvantage often leads to more extensive discussion.

Variations
- **Social Learning** – Learners play in pairs or teams.
- **Stick or Twist** – Learners have the chance to roll the dice a second time. However, if they do, they must take the number rolled on the second occasion.

Pros and Cons Dice
Rules of the game

Preparation
Play in groups of 3-5. Each group needs a set of **Pros and Cons cards**, a dice and a timer (e.g. mobile phone).

How to play
Player A turns over the top card and reads it out. She then throws the dice. The number on the dice will tell Player A how many advantages or disadvantages she must name. One of the other players starts the stopwatch and Player A has a minute to name the advantages/disadvantages. If Player A succeeds, she scores one point for each advantage/disadvantage named. If Player A does not succeed, she scores no points. Player B goes next.

For example
Player A turns over the following card:

> disadvantages of living in a big city

She rolls the dice and gets 4. Player A now has one minute to think of four disadvantages of living in a big city. If she succeeds, she scores four points.

How to win
The game finishes when all the cards have been used. The player with the highest score at the end of the game wins.

If...
- If you can't think of the required number of advantages or disadvantages, the next player can steal all your points by naming the remaining advantages or disadvantages.
- If all the other players agree that one of your advantages or disadvantages isn't relevant or is too similar to another advantage/disadvantage, you must try again.

Question Poker

Time	15–40 minutes
Interaction	Groups of 4–7 learners
Level	B1 (Intermediate) to C1 (Advanced)

Language areas practised

Sub-skills and Functions
- recalling specific information accurately
- expressing feelings and desires

Grammar and Lexis
- verb patterns
- future forms

Preparation
Photocopy the **Rules of the game** and the **Personalisation question cards** from page 117 of the Resource bank (one of each per group). Cut up the Question cards as indicated. Take a few extra pencils into class in case some of your learners don't have any. Before they start playing, do a quick demonstration with one group playing and the others watching.

Notes
Groups of five or six are best. For short games or at lower levels, give each group enough questions for two each (eight questions to a group of four). For longer games, higher levels or groups that know each other well, give each group enough questions for four each. If you think the learners might know each other's handwriting, get them to complete their answers in capital letters.

Question Poker — Rules of the game

Preparation
Play in groups of 4-7. Each group needs one set of **Question cards**, and one pencil each. Distribute the Question cards evenly among the players. Each player should write their answer to each question on the back of the card in pencil, keeping their answers secret. When everyone has finished, one player should collect and shuffle all the cards together without looking at them. He then spreads them all out on the table so that the questions are facing up and the answers are hidden.

How to play
Player A takes a Question card and looks at the answer without showing or telling the others. She should guess who wrote the answer and ask the question to this player. If the player she asks gives the answer on the card, Player A wins the card. If the player she asks doesn't give this answer, she replaces the card on the table with the question face up. Player B now takes a Question card and asks another player. You can't pick up your own cards.

How to win
The player who wins the most Question cards by the end of the game is the winner.

If…
- If someone asks you a question you wrote the answer to, you must provide the answer you wrote on the card.
- If, by chance, a player provides the answer on the card but didn't write the answer, you still win the card.

© Delta Publishing 2014 — SPEAKING GAMES by Jason Anderson

Section 2: Card Games

Regrets

Time	15–25 minutes
Interaction	Whole class
Level	B2 (Upper Intermediate) to C1 (Advanced)

Language areas practised

Sub-skills and Functions

- expressing regret and/or criticism
- peer-correcting formal errors

Grammar and Lexis

- 3rd conditional structures
- mixed conditional structures
- *should have* + past participle for criticism/regret
- *I wish… / If only…* structures

Preparation

Photocopy the **Rules of the game** (one per pair) and the **Regret cards** from page 121 of the Resource bank (one per learner). If you've only got a small class (under eight learners), you could give each learner two cards. This game can be used to practise several structures (see four examples under Grammar and Lexis above).

Depending on which structure you want to practise, provide an example before the game begins. The example given in the Rules of the game is 3rd conditional. It would also be possible to respond to this prompt with: *'You should have bought a ticket'*. See Variations below for how to use the cards with *If only…* and *I wish…* structures.

Notes

This is a simple mingle prompt activity that encourages accurate language use and provides an incentive for peer correction (see 'If…' rules). This is very useful with formally challenging grammar. If you want to include mixed conditionals, the six cards at the bottom of the sheet (text is in bold) should elicit a mixed conditional response. For example, *'If you'd had a cup of coffee, you'd feel more alert now'*.

Variations

- ***If only… / I wish…*** – For this structure, learners should change '*I*' to '*you*' and '*my*' to '*your*' on the Regret cards before they mingle.
- **Green Variation** – Don't copy the Rules of the game, just explain them and provide or elicit an example.

Regrets   Rules of the game

Preparation

Play as a whole class. You each need a **Regret card**. This is your regret. Think of a few ways that somebody would respond to it. For example:

Regret:

> I didn't buy a ticket for the train last week. I got caught and had to pay a fine!

Suitable response:

'If you'd bought a ticket, you wouldn't have paid a fine.'

If you like, you can write down one or two possible responses.

How to play

Stand up and mingle with the other learners in the class. When you meet another learner, read out your regret to them, but don't show the card. They should respond with a suitable answer. Listen to the answer carefully. If it's grammatically correct, award them one point. Then find another learner. Continue in this way, mingling and talking to different learners. Work in pairs only, not groups. Keep note of your own score.

How to win

The player with the most points at the end of the game wins.

If…

- If another learner makes a grammatical mistake in their answer, give them a clue where the mistake was, and get them to correct it. If you do, you both get a point!

SPEAKING GAMES by Jason Anderson   © Delta Publishing 2014

True Secrets

Time	30–60 minutes
Interaction	Whole class
Level	B1 (Intermediate) to C1 (Advanced)

Language areas practised

Sub-skills and Functions
- asking and answering improvised questions
- inventing information quickly

Grammar and Lexis
- question forms
- personal information

Preparation

Photocopy the **Rules of the game** (one per pair), the **True Secrets worksheet** (one per learner) and the **My True Secret cards** (one card per learner). Cut up the My True Secret cards as indicated. Take a few extra pencils into class if you think the learners may easily guess each other's pen colour. At lower levels, take the learners through the stages yourself and ask a few check questions before they begin the mingle.

Notes

This is a great icebreaker activity that can be played with five learners or more. If you only have five learners, take part yourself to make the numbers up to six. Groups of three are fine during the mingle activity - as long as there are seven or more learners. If you have over 14 learners, create two separate mingle groups. Before they begin, make sure the learners understand the importance of not revealing which is their True Secret until the end of the game (i.e. they shouldn't reveal it to each person they speak to). When redistributing the True Secret cards, if by chance you give a learner back their own card, just swap it for another.

In small classes, by the process of deduction, one of the learners is likely to guess everyone's true secret in c. 10 – 15 minutes. In large classes this will take longer, but you can stop the game at any point and get them to complete the True Secret column on the worksheet before finding out the truth.

True Secrets — Rules of the game

Preparation

Play as a whole class. Your teacher will give you a **True Secret card**. Without letting anybody else see, complete it with a <u>true</u> fact about you that nobody else knows, or could guess. Write in capital letters and use a pencil or black pen so that nobody can recognise your handwriting. Example ideas:

'I HAVE A TATTOO ON MY BACK.'
'I USED TO HAVE A PET RAT.'
'I CAN'T SWIM.'
'I FAILED MY DRIVING TEST 3 TIMES.'

Give your completed card to your teacher. Don't forget what you wrote! This is your 'True Secret'.

Your teacher will now give you somebody else's True Secret card. This is your 'New Secret'. Don't let anyone see it – read it, memorise it and put it in your pocket. You now have two secrets: the one you wrote, and the one you received.

The teacher will give you a **True Secret worksheet**. Complete it with the names of the other learners in the class.

How to play

Everybody stands and talks to other learners in pairs. When you meet another learner, tell each other your two secrets, but don't say which one is your True Secret. Your partner will ask you some questions about each of your secrets. Answer them (you will have to lie about your New Secret). Make a note of your partner's secrets on your worksheet. Complete the **True Secret column** when you know which of the secrets is true.

How to win

At the end of the game, try to guess each learner's True Secret and write these in the True Secret column. Everybody reveals which is their True Secret, and the learner who has guessed the most True Secrets is the winner.

If…

- If you are sure you know everybody's True Secret before the game finishes, shout out 'Stop!'. If you're right, you're the winner!

True Secrets

Worksheet

Section 3: Secrets & Lies

Stand up and mingle with your classmates. Find a partner, tell each other your two secrets and ask some questions about each of their secrets. Try to guess which one is their 'True Secret' and write it in the True Secret column. Don't let anyone else see the answers in your True Secret column. If you are confident that you have guessed everyone's True Secret, shout out 'STOP!' to end the game.

Name	1st secret	2nd secret	True Secret

SPEAKING GAMES by Jason Anderson © Delta Publishing 2014

True Secrets — My True Secret cards

Section 3: Secrets & Lies

MY TRUE SECRET
Complete this card in CAPITAL LETTERS so nobody can recognise your handwriting! Choose a secret that no-one else can guess about you:

MY TRUE SECRET
Complete this card in CAPITAL LETTERS so nobody can recognise your handwriting! Choose a secret that no-one else can guess about you:

MY TRUE SECRET
Complete this card in CAPITAL LETTERS so nobody can recognise your handwriting! Choose a secret that no-one else can guess about you:

MY TRUE SECRET
Complete this card in CAPITAL LETTERS so nobody can recognise your handwriting! Choose a secret that no-one else can guess about you:

MY TRUE SECRET
Complete this card in CAPITAL LETTERS so nobody can recognise your handwriting! Choose a secret that no-one else can guess about you:

MY TRUE SECRET
Complete this card in CAPITAL LETTERS so nobody can recognise your handwriting! Choose a secret that no-one else can guess about you:

MY TRUE SECRET
Complete this card in CAPITAL LETTERS so nobody can recognise your handwriting! Choose a secret that no-one else can guess about you:

MY TRUE SECRET
Complete this card in CAPITAL LETTERS so nobody can recognise your handwriting! Choose a secret that no-one else can guess about you:

MY TRUE SECRET
Complete this card in CAPITAL LETTERS so nobody can recognise your handwriting! Choose a secret that no-one else can guess about you:

MY TRUE SECRET
Complete this card in CAPITAL LETTERS so nobody can recognise your handwriting! Choose a secret that no-one else can guess about you:

MY TRUE SECRET
Complete this card in CAPITAL LETTERS so nobody can recognise your handwriting! Choose a secret that no-one else can guess about you:

MY TRUE SECRET
Complete this card in CAPITAL LETTERS so nobody can recognise your handwriting! Choose a secret that no-one else can guess about you:

MY TRUE SECRET
Complete this card in CAPITAL LETTERS so nobody can recognise your handwriting! Choose a secret that no-one else can guess about you:

MY TRUE SECRET
Complete this card in CAPITAL LETTERS so nobody can recognise your handwriting! Choose a secret that no-one else can guess about you:

MY TRUE SECRET
Complete this card in CAPITAL LETTERS so nobody can recognise your handwriting! Choose a secret that no-one else can guess about you:

MY TRUE SECRET
Complete this card in CAPITAL LETTERS so nobody can recognise your handwriting! Choose a secret that no-one else can guess about you:

© Delta Publishing 2014 — SPEAKING GAMES by Jason Anderson

Truth or Lie

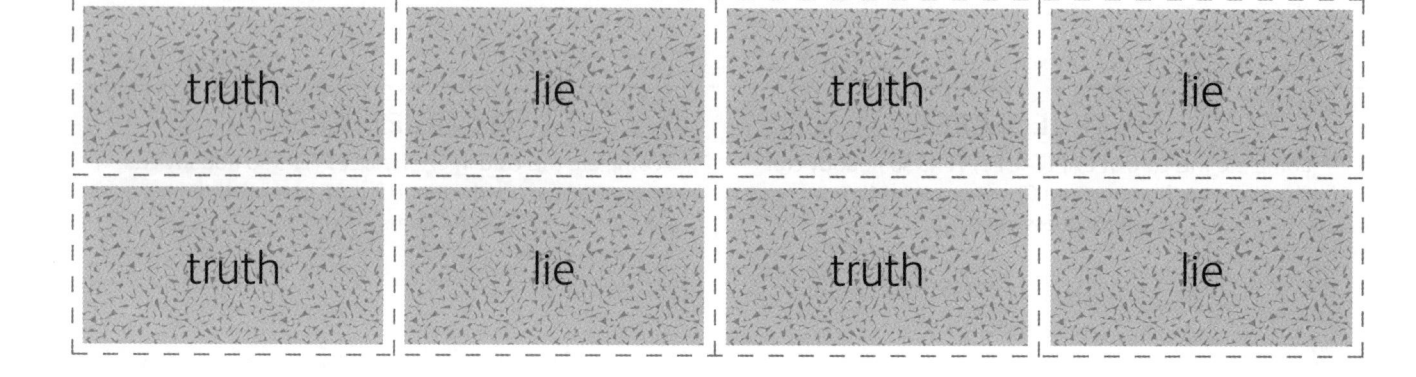

Time	20–40 minutes
Interaction	Groups of 3–5 learners
Level	B1 (Intermediate) to C1 (Advanced)

Language areas practised

Sub-skills and Functions
- making short, unprepared speaking turns
- inventing information quickly
- analysing a spoken text critically

Grammar and Lexis
- past simple
- reported (indirect) speech

Preparation
Photocopy the **Rules of the game**, the **Game board** and the **Truth or Lie cards** (one copy of each per group). Cut up the cards as indicated. Players will need one counter each (e.g. coins).

Notes
Depending on your learners and how much time you have, you can let them vary how they play. Some groups will naturally start asking questions to the player who is speaking, others will choose not to. Make sure each player moves forward one square at the start of their turn so that they are talking about a new topic. Learners often make use of reported speech when analysing each other's summaries, e.g. *'He said that he had been to Italy, but…'*.

Variations
- **Higher Levels** – Players are allowed to ask three questions to the speaker after the initial answer, or the speaker has to speak for one minute before they decide whether it's the truth or a lie.

Truth or Lie — Rules of the game

Preparation
Play in groups of 3-5. Each group needs a set of **Truth or Lie cards** and all players need a counter (e.g. coins). Shuffle the cards and place them face down in a pile on the Game board.

How to play
Player A moves forward one square and picks up a **Truth or Lie card**, keeping it secret from the other players. She must then talk about the topic on the square she landed on. If her card says: *'Truth'*, she must tell the truth. If the card says: *'Lie'*, she must lie about the topic. When she has finished, the other players must discuss and agree on whether she was telling the truth or lying. Then she reveals her card before putting it at the bottom of the pile of cards. If the others guessed correctly, her turn finishes. If they guessed wrongly, she moves forward, takes another Truth or Lie card and talks about the topic on the new square. Again the other players must guess *'truth'* or *'lie'*. Player B goes next by moving forward one square.

How to win
The first player to reach Finish is the winner!

If…
- If the others can't agree whether you are telling the truth or lying, the person on your right should decide.
- If you deceive your classmates three times in a single turn, your turn ends and the next player takes her turn. Thus, you can move forward a maximum of three squares in a turn.

Truth or Lie — Cards

truth	lie	truth	lie
truth	lie	truth	lie

SPEAKING GAMES by Jason Anderson © Delta Publishing 2014

Truth or Lie

Game board

Section 3: Secrets & Lies

FINISH

- the shoes you are wearing now
- the last text message you sent
- your favourite website
- a picture on your wall at home
- a habit that you have recently given up
- the last book you read
- the most enjoyable thing you did last year
- the first time you went on holiday without your parents
- the first person you fell in love with
- the first pop group / singer that you really got into
- your favourite subject at school
- family holidays when you were a child
- your favourite childhood game
- your first memory

all players start here

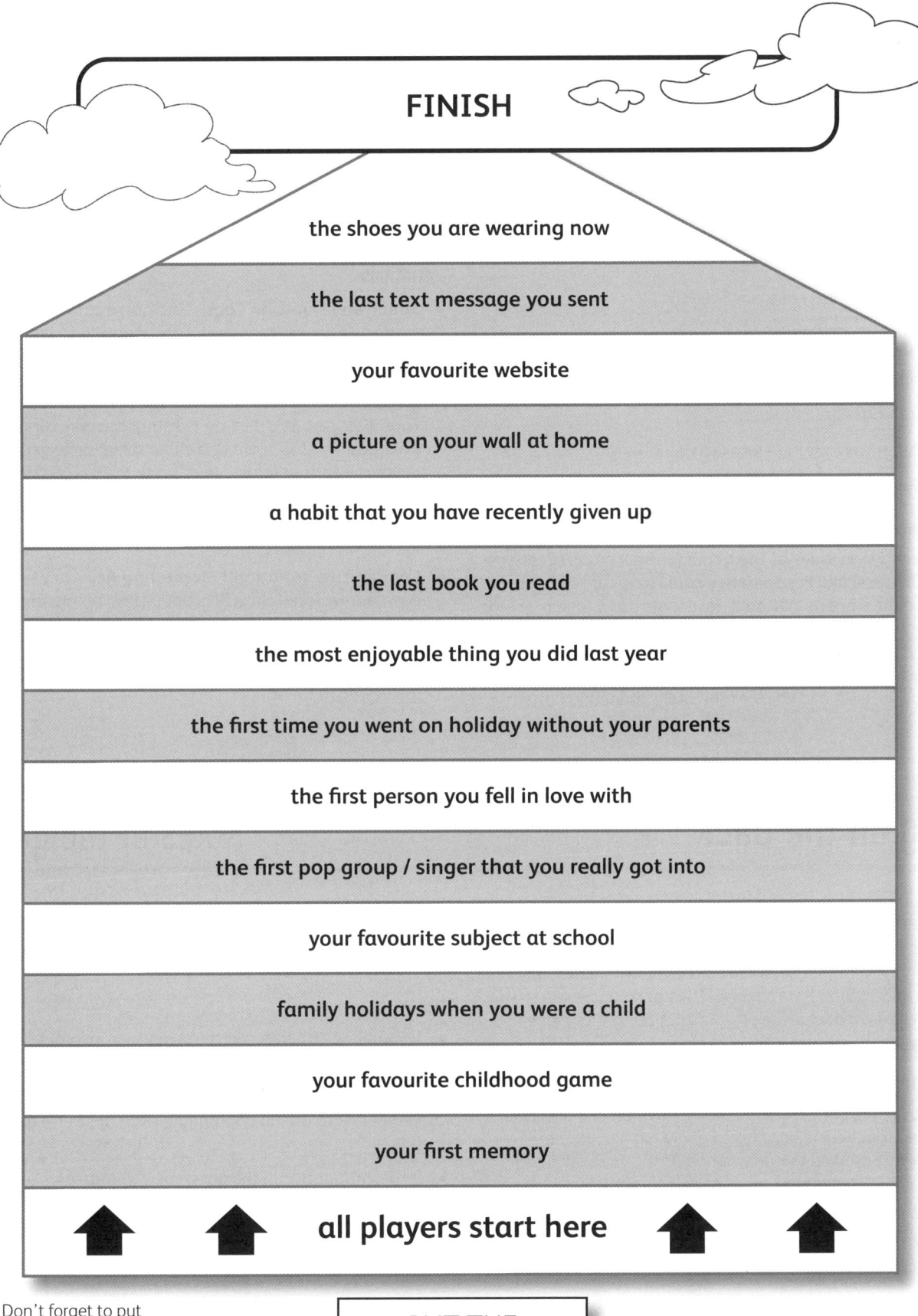

Don't forget to put used cards to the bottom of the pile

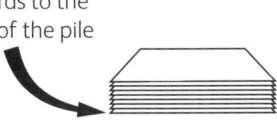

PUT THE TRUTH OR LIE CARDS HERE

© Delta Publishing 2014

SPEAKING GAMES by Jason Anderson

Section 3: Secrets & Lies

Tag on the Back

Time	15–25 minutes
Interaction	Whole class
Level	B1 (Intermediate) to C1 (Advanced)

Language areas practised

Sub-skills and Functions

- making guesses
- using intonation to sound friendly
- correcting misconceptions

Grammar and Lexis

- question tags
- 'same-way' question tags (see Variations)
- use of *actually* to correct factual errors

Preparation

Photocopy the **Rules of the game** (one per group of three or four learners) and the **Sentence cards** (one card per learner). Cut up the cards as indicated. Take some sticky tape or safety pins into class to stick the 'tags' on the learners' backs. If you have a large class, you can repeat some of the cards. This game follows on nicely from work on question tags. Before you begin, elicit and drill the most likely intonation pattern for 'conversational question tags'. Also drill an appropriate intonation pattern for *'Actually…'* when used to correct a misconception (high fall with slight rise at end).

Notes

Do a couple of examples before the game starts to show how to ask and respond to the tag questions. This game works well without being competitive and can be concluded when the faster learners have finished. If you want a winner, see *Variations* below.

Variations

- **Same-way Question Tags** – The game can also be used to practise use of 'same-way tags', surprisingly common among proficient speakers, but rarely taught in textbooks. This is where the tag is not inverted and the question is asked to show interest, e.g. *'You speak French, do you? That must be useful!'* Same-way tags are only common after positive statements, so either remove the negative Sentence cards or remind learners to use inverted tags as normal for negative statements. The basic game synopsis is similar, with the tags being used to begin a quick conversation.

- **Competitive Variation / Monitoring Accuracy** – Give each learner three chips (e.g. paperclips) before they start playing. They can win chips off each other if they spot and successfully correct mistakes in each other's tag questions. The learner with the most chips at the end of the activity is the winner.

Tag on the Back   Rules of the game

Preparation

Play as a whole class. Your teacher will give you a **Sentence card** for you to complete. You can do this with either **true** or *false* information – you choose. Then get a classmate to stick your completed sentence on your back using sticky tape or a safety pin. You are now ready to play.

How to play

Stand up and mingle around the room. Approach another learner from behind, read his card and tap him on the shoulder. Based on the information on the card, ask a tag question to confirm the information. For example:

   'You live in Verona, don't you?'
   'You don't like olives, do you?'

Choose your auxiliary verb carefully. Try to develop the exchange into a short conversation (1-2 minutes), then conclude it and move on.

If…

- If somebody taps you on the shoulder, turn around and respond to his question.

- If the information in the question is true, confirm it. Remember to use an appropriate short answer, e.g. *'Yes, I do.'*

- If the information in the question is wrong, say: *'Actually,…'* and correct the statement, e.g. *'Actually, I don't.'*

Tag on the Back

Sentence cards

I live in _____.	I'm from _____.	I went to _____ on Saturday.
I can speak _____.	I've been to _____.	I'm living in _____ at the moment.
I didn't come to the lesson on _____.	I don't like _____.	I'm not _____ today.
I want to _____ next year.	I can't _____.	I have to _____ tomorrow.
I'm working at _____ at the moment.	I was _____ing in _____ this morning.	I've got _____.
I've _____ since _____.	I'm going to _____ this evening.	I won't _____ if it rains tomorrow.
I forgot to _____ last week.	I haven't got _____.	I couldn't _____ two weeks ago.

Section 3: Secrets & Lies

Question Taboo

Time	15–30 minutes
Interaction	Whole class
Level	B1 (Intermediate) to C1 (Advanced)

Language areas practised

Sub-skills and Functions

- paraphrasing
- reformulating an idea

Grammar and Lexis

- present simple tense
- personal information

Preparation

Photocopy the **Rules of the game** (one for each pair) and the **Question cards** (one card per learner). Cut up the Question cards as indicated. If you have over 18 learners, use some of the questions twice. The rules of the game are fairly easy (see Green Variation below), but it's a good idea to use one of the cards to do an example, with a learner asking the question and you trying to answer it. Pretend you don't know the TABOO word the first time you answer and use it to elicit the *'Taboo!'* response.

Notes

Question Taboo makes a good icebreaker mingle activity for a new class, but works equally well with classes that know each other. It gives learners useful practice in reformulating ideas or paraphrasing a familiar concept. You should keep scores on the board, preparing a column for each learner. Get them to report their scores after each exchange.

Variations

- **Green Variation** – Explain the rules rather than copying the Rules of the game. This saves on photocopying costs and cutting up time!
- **No Scores** – If your class is not very competitive, they might prefer to play without keeping score.

Question Taboo

Rules of the game

Preparation

Play as a whole class. Your teacher will give each of you a different **Question card**. Don't show it to anyone. On the card is a common question. There is also a 'TABOO' word. Keep this word secret.

How to play

Stand up and find a partner. Ask each other your questions. You must try to answer your partner's question without using her TABOO word. The problem is that you don't know what this word is!

If you use your partner's TABOO word, your partner will say: *'Taboo!'* You can try to answer the question three times, and each time your partner will say: *'Taboo'* if you use the word. When you have both answered each other's questions, tell your teacher your score (see 'If...' rules) and find another partner. Try to talk to all the other learners in the class. Remember never to let anybody see your own TABOO word.

If...

- If you answer a question successfully the first time without using the TABOO word, you score three points.
- If you answer a question without using the TABOO word the second time, you score two points.
- If you answer a question without using the TABOO word the third time, you score one point.
- If you fail to answer the question without using the TABOO word the 3rd time, you score no points. Move on and try again!

How to win

The player who scores the most points by the end of the game is the winner. Your teacher will keep score.

Question Taboo

Question cards

Section 3: Secrets & Lies

Your question is...	Your question is...	Your question is...
How long have you been studying English here?	How old are you?	What do you do?
Your TABOO word is...	**Your TABOO word is...**	**Your TABOO word is...**
since	am	a

Your question is...	Your question is...	Your question is...
Where do you come from?	How do you spend your free time?	What's your favourite movie?
Your TABOO word is...	**Your TABOO word is...**	**Your TABOO word is...**
from	like	I (pronoun)

Your question is...	Your question is...	Your question is...
How many brothers and sisters do you have?	Where do you live?	What's your favourite food?
Your TABOO word is...	**Your TABOO word is...**	**Your TABOO word is...**
and	in	like

Your question is...	Your question is...	Your question is...
What is your name?	What are you doing tonight?	What kind of music do you like?
Your TABOO word is...	**Your TABOO word is...**	**Your TABOO word is...**
my	go	listen

Your question is...	Your question is...	Your question is...
What do your parents do?	Do you like this school?	How are you today?
Your TABOO word is...	**Your TABOO word is...**	**Your TABOO word is...**
my	it	fine

Your question is...	Your question is...	Your question is...
What's your favourite website?	Why did you take this English course?	How did you get to school today?
Your TABOO word is...	**Your TABOO word is...**	**Your TABOO word is...**
don't	want	by

© Delta Publishing 2014 — SPEAKING GAMES by Jason Anderson

Truth Mingle

Time	30–50 minutes
Interaction	Groups of 3–5 learners
Level	B1 (Intermediate) to C1 (Advanced)

Language areas practised

Sub-skills and Functions

- identifying things in common
- speculating on possible future events
- enquiring about future plans
- describing future plans

Grammar and Lexis

- future perfect
- future continuous
- present continuous / *going to* for future arrangements/intentions

Preparation

Photocopy the **Rules of the game** and the **Statement list** (one of each per group). You'll need at least six learners in your class to play *Truth Mingle*. If you divide them into just two groups, the groups simply swap Statement lists after completing them. If you've got three or more groups, get each group to pass their Statement list to the group on their left. For example, with three groups, give group A's Statement list to group B, group B's Statement list to group C and group C's to group A.

During the preparation stage, remind the learners that they can write as many false statements as they like.

Notes

There are several stages to this activity and you should explain each stage before you begin. It is likely that learners will use future forms naturally during all the stages, not only during the *Truth Mingle* itself. Four of the statements 'force' the learner to use the future perfect (2 & 6) and future continuous (3 & 5). For the remaining two statements, the present continuous and *going to* forms are both possible.

Timings for each stage of the activity are difficult to predict and will depend on your learners, so keep it flexible if possible. Keep the actual *Truth Mingle* in Stage 3 short (2-4 minutes) to encourage careful planning in Stage 2 and to ensure the need for some speculation during Stage 4.

Variations

- **Other Tenses** – This game can be used to practise almost any verb grammar in English (narrative tenses, present perfect, modal verbs, etc.). Either change the statements to 'force' your required tense(s) or instruct the learners to use a specific tense or tenses.

Truth Mingle

Rules of the game

Preparation
Play in groups of 3-5. Your teacher will give you a **Statement list** with six statements about your group members' plans for next week. Complete each statement with information that can be true (i.e. real plans) or false. Keep the correct answers secret from other groups. Don't write anything in the 'True or False?' column.

Stage 1
Your teacher will give you the Statement list from another group. Discuss quickly which statements you think are true future plans and which are false.

Stage 2
The *Truth Mingle* in Stage 3 only lasts for a few minutes. Before it begins, you have a few minutes to prepare in your group. Decide who will interview whom about what.

Stage 3
During the *Truth Mingle* stage, the following rules apply:

- you can ask questions to anyone in the class, but you can only talk to one person at a time
- everybody must tell the truth
- you can only ask a person about their own plans
- you can't ignore or avoid a question

Stage 4
Get back together as a group and make your final decisions about which statements are true and which are false. Complete the 'True or False?' column.

How to win
Each team reads out their statements, saying which are true, which are false and why they think this. The team who gets the most correct wins!

Truth Mingle

Statement list

Group Name: _____

Next Week...	True or False?
1. On _____ day, two members of our group are _____	
2. By the end of the week, everybody in our group will have _____	
3. Next week, nobody in our group will be ____ing _____	
4. On _____day, one member of our group is _____	
5. At the weekend, we will all be ____ing _____	
6. By Wednesday, two of us will have _____	

Gotcha!

Time	15–30 minutes
Interaction	Whole class
Level	B1 (Intermediate) to B2 (Upper Intermediate)

Language areas practised

Sub-skills and Functions
- improvising questions
- leading a conversation

Grammar and Lexis
- question forms
- food and drink (or any lexical area – see Variations below)

Preparation
Photocopy the **Rules of the game** (one per group of 3–4 learners) and the **'Gotcha!' cards** (one card per learner). Cut up the cards as indicated. If your group are at a lower level, select words they know. Teach them the word *'Gotcha!'* and explain that it is a contraction of *'I've got you.'* – often used by children to indicate that they have caught somebody when playing chasing games.

Notes
The 'Gotcha!' words are all on the topic of food and drink. This will 'force' the learners to begin discussing this topic. You can create your own 'Gotcha!' words to practise any lexical area you wish (work and jobs, money and finance, adjectives of personality, etc.).

Variations
- Create your own 'Gotcha!' cards to practise any lexical area you have studied recently.
- **Green Variation** – Don't copy the Rules of the game, just show them on a projector or explain them.

Gotcha! — Rules of the game

Preparation
Play as a whole class. Your teacher will give each of you a different **'Gotcha!' card**. On your card is a word. Memorise this word and put it in your pocket. Every learner has a different word. Some are verbs, some are nouns and some are adjectives. All are common words.

How to play
You are at a party. Mingle and meet all the others at the party. Your aim is to get everybody to say your word. However you can't say the word yourself, so you will need to lead them to the word with questions or conversation. At the same time, they will be trying to get you to say their 'Gotcha!' word.

How to win
The player who scores the most points by the end of the game wins.

If…
- If someone says your word, say: *'Gotcha!'* and show them your 'Gotcha!' word. Don't say it or let anybody else see it. The teacher will give you a point.
- If you find out another player's 'Gotcha!' word, don't tell anyone else – that will make it too easy for them, and they're your competitors!

Gotcha! — Cards

Your Gotcha! word: **fruit**	Your Gotcha! word: **fry**	Your Gotcha! word: **chef**
Your Gotcha! word: **restaurant**	Your Gotcha! word: **menu**	Your Gotcha! word: **sweet**
Your Gotcha! word: **cocktail**	Your Gotcha! word: **fast food**	Your Gotcha! word: **taste**
Your Gotcha! word: **recipe**	Your Gotcha! word: **spaghetti**	Your Gotcha! word: **hungry**
Your Gotcha! word: **waiter**	Your Gotcha! word: **oven**	Your Gotcha! word: **ice**
Your Gotcha! word: **hamburger**	Your Gotcha! word: **delicious**	Your Gotcha! word: **chicken**

Section 3: Secrets & Lies

© Delta Publishing 2014 — SPEAKING GAMES by Jason Anderson

Secret Sentences

Time	20–40 minutes
Interaction	Groups of 3–5 learners
Level	B1 (Intermediate) to C1 (Advanced)

Language areas practised

Sub-skills and Functions

- agreeing and disagreeing
- challenging someone's opinion
- eliciting agreement

Grammar and Lexis

- Spoken discourse markers: 'Actually…', 'To be honest…', 'What's more…'

Preparation

Photocopy the **Rules of the game**, the **Secret Sentence cards** (on next page) and the **Opinion cards** from page 116 of the Resource bank (one of each per group). Cut up the cards as indicated. Remove any Opinion cards that you feel may be unsuitable for your learners. Check the remaining ones for vocabulary that may need to be pre-taught (e.g. *be banned*).

Notes

You may want to pre-teach some of the spoken discourse markers used on the secret sentence cards before the discussions: *Actually; To be honest; In fact; What's more; Well; Sorry*; etc.

Variations

- After playing the game once, learners can write their own secret sentences. For example, they can personalise them to their class, by including individual catchphrases or each other's names. Bear in mind that each group will have to create secret sentences for a different group. You need 10-20 secret sentences per group.
- You can extend the length of the individual discussions to 10 or 20 minutes if you prefer. If you do, each learner can take two, three or more secret sentences at the start of the discussion. If they lose a sentence, they take another from the pile. The remaining rules apply.

Secret Sentences   Rules of the game

Preparation

Play in groups of 3-5. Each group needs a set of **Opinion cards** and **Secret Sentence cards**. Place the cards in two separate piles, both face down. Each player should take a Secret Sentence card, memorise the sentence and keep it in their hand, making sure no-one else sees it. Prepare a timer (e.g. mobile phone) to time discussions for five minutes each.

How to play

Turn over the first Opinion card and discuss the topic for five minutes. Try to use your Secret Sentence in the discussion so that no-one notices. After five minutes, conclude your discussion and find out who has used their secret sentence. If you used your secret sentence without anyone noticing, you win the card – keep it and take a new Secret Sentence card from the pile. Start a new discussion by turning over the next Opinion card.

How to win

The player who has won the most Secret Sentence cards by the end of the game wins. Keep the cards you have won separate from your current Secret Sentence card.

If…

- If you think someone has just said their secret sentence, say: *'Secret sentence!'* If you're right, you win the card – take it from the other player, who should take a new Secret Sentence card from the pile.
- If you say: *'Secret sentence!'* and you're wrong, the person who you challenged wins your Secret Sentence card and you take another one from the top of the pile!
- If you didn't manage to use your Secret Sentence at the end of a discussion, you should keep it.

Secret Sentences

Sentence cards

Section 3: Secrets & Lies

YOUR SECRET SENTENCE:
> I think we should look at the facts more carefully.

YOUR SECRET SENTENCE:
> Actually, you've got a good point.

YOUR SECRET SENTENCE:
> That doesn't mean it's true.

YOUR SECRET SENTENCE:
> Sorry, can you prove that?

YOUR SECRET SENTENCE:
> Every word you've said has been completely untrue.

YOUR SECRET SENTENCE:
> Sorry, I forgot what I was saying.

YOUR SECRET SENTENCE:
> I don't disagree, but I don't agree either.

YOUR SECRET SENTENCE:
> I'd like to raise a new point here.

YOUR SECRET SENTENCE:
> Sorry, can I say something, please?

YOUR SECRET SENTENCE:
> Does anybody know what I mean?

YOUR SECRET SENTENCE:
> Are you making this up?

YOUR SECRET SENTENCE:
> To be honest, I don't know enough about it.

YOUR SECRET SENTENCE:
> What's more, the situation is getting worse.

YOUR SECRET SENTENCE:
> Well, that's partially true, but only partially.

YOUR SECRET SENTENCE:
> In fact, the exact opposite is true.

YOUR SECRET SENTENCE:
> Actually, you've just convinced me.

YOUR SECRET SENTENCE:
> That's definitely not true.

YOUR SECRET SENTENCE:
> You've been very quiet – what do you think?

YOUR SECRET SENTENCE:
> Please don't interrupt me.

YOUR SECRET SENTENCE:
> This discussion is really boring!

YOUR SECRET SENTENCE:
> One thing we haven't talked about yet is money.

© Delta Publishing 2014 · SPEAKING GAMES by Jason Anderson

Section 3: Secrets & Lies

This Weekend

Time	15–30 minutes
Interaction	Pairs or small groups
Level	B1 (Intermediate) to C1 (Advanced)

Language areas practised

Sub-skills and Functions

- describing future plans and arrangements
- interviewing someone

Grammar and Lexis

- *going to* for future plans
- present continuous for future arrangements

Preparation

Photocopy the **Rules of the game** (one for each pair or group) and the **Planning table** (one per learner). The game can be played in pairs for a short warmer, or in larger groups of 3-4 for a longer game.

Notes

In order to make it possible to discover the lie, make sure the learners understand that one of their plans must be a complete lie; this should correspond to the information they write in one of the five boxes on their Planning table. A teacher example will demonstrate what kind of language they'll need (mainly *be going to* + verb and present continuous, but *will* and present simple for future are also possible). It will also show them how to lie effectively!

Variations

- **Green Variation** – Don't copy anything! Explain the rules verbally or display them using a projector, and get the learners to draw their own tables in their notebooks.

- **Whole Class Variation** – Each learner prepares as already described. Then they all write their name on their Planning table and stick them on the walls of the classroom. They go round for 5-10 minutes, looking at each other's plans and taking notes if they wish (no questions at this stage). For the final stage, each player sits in a 'hot seat' in front of the other players, summarises their weekend, and then answers questions before others guess which is the lie. This option also lends itself to a team game, with teams consulting before agreeing which is the lie.

This Weekend

Preparation

Play in pairs or small groups. You are going to tell each other about five plans you have for the coming weekend. Four will be true, and one will be a lie. The aim of the game is to discover each other's lies. Before you begin, use the **Planning table** to make notes on your plans (five minutes). Remember to keep the lie a secret. Also think about what tenses you will need to describe future arrangements and plans.

How to play

Player A goes first. She gives a summary of her weekend, including all five plans. The other player(s) then ask her

Rules of the game

questions about her plans and try to guess which one is the lie. They can look at the notes on her Planning table as they do this. Player B goes next.

If...

- If you guess a player's lie correctly, you win one point.
- If you're playing in groups and nobody guesses a player's lie, the 'liar' wins three points.

How to win

The player with the most points at the end of the game is the winner.

This Weekend

Planning table

Plan your weekend here. The information in **one** of the five boxes **must be completely untrue**. The information in the other four boxes **must all be true**:

Friday evening	
Saturday morning	
Saturday afternoon / evening	
Sunday morning	
Sunday afternoon / evening	

This Weekend

Planning table

Plan your weekend here. The information in **one** of the five boxes **must be completely untrue**. The information in the other four boxes **must all be true**:

Friday evening	
Saturday morning	
Saturday afternoon / evening	
Sunday morning	
Sunday afternoon / evening	

Passive Porkies

Time	30–50 minutes
Interaction	Pairs
Level	B1 (Intermediate) to C1 (Advanced)

Language areas practised

Sub-skills and Functions
- improvising responses to questions
- describing recent events
- asking follow-up questions

Grammar and Lexis
- passive forms (including present simple, past simple and present perfect passive)
- question forms

Preparation

Photocopy the **Question worksheet** (one per learner). The learners will benefit from a demonstration of this game. Get them to ask you a few of the questions and then try to guess which of your answers were true and which were not. You can use this opportunity to sort out any issues with the question forms and possible follow-up questions. Take learners through the stages of this activity as a whole class (preparation, game, scoring).

Notes

'*To tell Porkies*' is a common slang expression used in London, UK. It means to tell lies and comes from Cockney rhyming slang where '*pork pies*' = lies. Your learners might be interested to learn this.

Encourage your learners to provide full sentence answers to the questions if you'd like to ensure that they practise using the passive forms during the game. It is likely that more natural use of passive forms will occur when learners are answering the follow-up questions and also when they are checking their answers at the end.

Variations

- **Lower Levels** – Learners just tell the truth to all the questions and focus their attention on getting the passive forms in their answers right.
- **Higher Levels** – Let them change any part of their questions, or replace them completely as long as they use passive forms.

Passive Porkies

Rules of the game

Preparation

Play in pairs. Before you begin, complete the 10 questions on the worksheet so that they are relevant to your partner. Add a follow-up question for each one. Leave the last column blank.

How to play

Take turns to ask and answer your questions. During the conversation some of your answers must be honest, and some of the answers (at least three) must be lies. If you lie, you should also lie to the follow-up questions. After each of your partner's answers, put a tick or a cross in the last column: put a tick if you think your partner told the truth and a cross if you think they lied. After you have asked all the questions, find out which of your partner's answers were lies.

How to win

You score one point for each answer you correctly guessed as a truth or a lie. The player with the highest score wins.

If...

- If you do know the answer to a question, you can choose to tell the truth or lie.
- If you don't know the answer to a question, just lie!

Passive Porkies

Question worksheet

Passive Question	Follow-up Question (e.g. When? Who by? What happened?)	?
1 Has your _____ (e.g. mobile phone) ever been stolen?		
2 What is your _____ (e.g. ring, bag) made from?		
3 How often is/are your _____ (e.g. room) cleaned?		
4 Who was/were your _____ (e.g. sunglasses, perfume) made by?		
5 What changes have been made to your _____ (e.g. Facebook status, hairstyle) over the last year?		
6 In which country was/were your _____ (e.g. T-shirt) made?		
7 Has your _____ (e.g. computer, motorbike) ever been repaired?		
8 When was your _____ (e.g. level of English, eyesight) last tested?		
9 What is the most interesting _____ (e.g. gossip, news) that has been posted by your friends this week?		
10 When was a _____ (e.g. present, warning) last given to you?		

Kangaroo Court

Time	40–60 minutes
Interaction	Groups of 3–5 learners
Level	B2 (Upper Intermediate) to C1 (Advanced)

Language areas practised

Sub-skills and Functions

- justifying past actions
- thinking creatively
- interrogating a suspect
- responding to accusations

Grammar and Lexis

- narrative tenses
- crime and courtroom

Preparation

Photocopy the **Rules of the game** and the **Crime cards** (one of each per group). Cut up the cards as indicated. Optimum group size is 4-5. Depending on time available, players can each stand trial once or twice. With lower-level classes, check key vocabulary before they begin (*sentence*; *stand trial*; *justify*; *the accused*; *blame*; *(suspended) community service*; *impersonate*; *acquit*; *witness*; *forge*).

Notes

This game turns the traditional ELT activity of matching sentences to crimes into a comical role play. The rather implausible synopsis encourages the learner standing trial to be as creative with her story as possible in order to receive a lenient sentence. It encourages quick thinking and rigorous interrogation. As always with free-flowing creative role plays, timings are very difficult to predict – so be flexible if possible!

Variations

- **Lower Levels** – Give each learner their Crime card in advance and allow 3-5 minutes for preparation.
- **Courtroom Drama** – Choose one card, read out the crime, assign roles to learners for a mock trial (judge, lawyers, defendant, etc.) and allow 10 minutes for all to prepare.

Kangaroo Court — Rules of the game

Preparation

Play in groups of 3-5. Your teacher will give you a set of **Crime cards**. Without looking at them, place them in a pile on the table.

Background Synopsis

You will take turns to stand trial in court for a crime described on one of the Crime cards. Unfortunately, the court's computer system has been damaged by a virus, so all other details of the crime have been lost. As the player on trial, you can tell the court what you want about the crime in order to justify it. You will have no time to prepare for the trial and don't know what the crime is until the trial begins. The court psychologist has checked the mental health of every player and reported no illnesses or problems of any kind.

How to play

Player A stands trial first. The other players take the top card, read out the crime and the maximum and minimum sentences. Without preparation, Player A must explain exactly what happened and why. The other players can ask as many questions as they want, and then must choose a sentence from the card. The player receives the corresponding score. Player B stands trial next.

How to win

The player who receives the lowest score for their crime(s) wins.

If…

- If you choose to blame somebody else for your crime, you must still stand trial along with the person you blamed – and play both roles. Both of you are then sentenced at the end of the trial and you score whichever sentence is the highest.

Kangaroo Court — Crime cards

Crime Card 1
You were arrested after trying to steal a British policeman's hat in London.

Sentence	Score
6 months in prison	5
3 months in prison	4
1 month in prison	3
fine of £1000 and 3 months' community service	2
fine of £500 and 2 months' community service	1

Crime Card 2
You were arrested for pretending to be a panda in a zoo.

Sentence	Score
6 months' community service	5
3 months' community service	4
1 month's community service	3
suspended community service	2
acquitted (no sentence)	1

Crime Card 3
You were arrested after you were caught on CCTV stealing toothpaste from a shop on four separate occasions.

Sentence	Score
1 month in prison	5
fine of £1000 and 3 months' community service	4
fine of £500 and 2 months' community service	3
1 month's community service	2
suspended community service	1

Crime Card 4
You were arrested at a hospital for trying to impersonate a doctor.

Sentence	Score
2 years in prison and £5,000 fine	5
1 year in prison and £5,000 fine	4
6 months in prison and £5,000 fine	3
3 months in prison and £5,000 fine	2
1 month in prison and £5,000 fine	1

Crime Card 5
You were arrested after biting a dog on the leg. The dog required veterinary treatment.

Sentence	Score
6 months' community service	5
3 months' community service	4
1 month's community service	3
suspended community service	2
acquitted (no sentence)	1

Crime Card 6
You were arrested after someone noticed you had 'borrowed' two live chickens from a farm for two weeks.

Sentence	Score
1 month in prison	5
fine of £1000 and 3 months' community service	4
fine of £500 and 2 months' community service	3
1 month's community service	2
suspended community service	1

Crime Card 7
You were arrested in a shop after you tried to buy four boxes of chocolates using a forged £50 note. Investigations showed the note was printed from your computer.

Sentence	Score
6 months in prison	5
3 months in prison	4
1 month in prison	3
fine of £1000 and 3 months' community service	2
fine of £500 and 2 months' community service	1

Crime Card 8
You were arrested for knocking down (in your car) and killing a robber who had just come out of a bank with £20,000 he had stolen.

Sentence	Score
25 years in prison	5
5 years in prison	4
6 months in prison	3
1 year's community service	2
acquitted (no sentence)	1

Crime Card 9
You were arrested for eating your best friend's wedding cake two hours before the wedding.

Sentence	Score
1 month in prison	5
fine of £1000 and 3 months' community service	4
fine of £500 and 2 months' community service	3
1 month's community service	2
suspended community service	1

Crime Card 10
You were arrested for hacking into the email account of a famous author.

Sentence	Score
3 months in prison	5
1 month in prison	4
fine of £1000 and 3 months' community service	3
fine of £500 and 2 months' community service	2
1 month's community service	1

© Delta Publishing 2014 — SPEAKING GAMES by Jason Anderson

Section 3: Secrets & Lies

Would I lie to you?

Time	10–60 minutes
Interaction	Groups of 4–7 learners
Level	B1 (Intermediate) to C1 (Advanced)

Language areas practised

Sub-skills and Functions

- asking questions / interrogating
- describing past experiences
- recalling an anecdote

Grammar and Lexis

- narrative tenses
- present perfect for life experience

Preparation

Photocopy the **Rules of the game** and the **Prompt cards** (one of each per group). Cut up the cards as indicated. Each player will need two cards per round, so if you want to play two rounds, double the number of copies. Depending on the size and level of the groups, a round can take anything from 10-30 minutes! However, it really doesn't matter if the players don't finish a round, they'll still enjoy practising their speaking skills and scoring points.

Notes

This game is based loosely on the UK TV show of the same name. It provides useful practice of narrative tenses through the questions and answers.

Variations

- **Green Variation** – No need to copy the Prompt cards. Use slips of recycled paper.
- **True to Life Variation** – You can play it as a whole class as on the TV show. Get each player to complete one card (no need for the Prompt cards) with a true, interesting life experience. Collect all these in, remembering who wrote what and add several of your own to the mix (e.g. *'I've met the president of my country.'* or *'I was once bitten by a venomous snake.'* etc.). The learners play in two teams with one learner taking a card from you and answering questions from the other team (it's your choice whether you give them back their real card or one of your added ones).

Would I lie to you?   Rules of the game

Preparation

Play in groups of 4-7. Your teacher will give you a set of **Prompt cards**. Each player should take two cards and complete one of them with true information (choosing something interesting), and the other card with false information (something you've never done!). Don't let anyone know which is true and which is a lie. When you have finished, put both cards face down in front of you (so no-one can read them).

How to play

Player A goes first. The player on his right chooses one of his cards and turns it over. Player A must now read the sentence on it. The other learners must ask questions to find out more information. For example: *'When did you do this?'*, *'Where?'*, *'Who with?'*, *'Why?'*, etc. When they are ready, the other players must decide whether the information is true or a lie. Then Player A reveals whether it is the truth or a lie. Each player who guessed correctly wins one point. If no-one guessed correctly, Player A wins three points. Player B goes next.

How to win

The player with the highest score at the end of the game wins.

If...

- If the card you have to talk about is not true, you should keep this secret! Pretend that it really happened and answer the questions realistically. You score more points if you deceive the other players.
- If the card you have to talk about is true, you must answer all the questions honestly.

SPEAKING GAMES by Jason Anderson   © Delta Publishing 2014

Would I lie to you? Prompt cards

I've eaten…	I've met…	I once lost…
I've worked as…	I once forgot to…	I once found…
I once bought…	I've driven…	I've written…
I once played…	I've travelled…	I once appeared on…
I once saw…	I've broken…	I once tried to…

Lie Auction

Time	30–50 minutes
Interaction	Whole class divided into an even number of teams
Level	B1 (Intermediate) to C1 (Advanced)

Language areas practised

Sub-skills and Functions
- describing abilities, past events and past habits
- hypothesising about possible abilities, events and habits
- asking questions

Grammar and Lexis
Any or all of the following:
- present perfect for life experience
- can / could for ability
- used to for past habits

Preparation
Photocopy the **Lie Auction worksheet** (one for each team). With small classes (under 12 learners), play as a whole class with just two teams. If you have 12 or more learners, create an even number of teams of 3-5 players. Each team then pairs up with another team for the playing stage. If you have very competitive learners, get each team to note down which of their statements are true or untrue on a separate piece of paper. This will reassure the players that other teams haven't changed an answer mid-game! They can do this at the end of the preparation stage.

Notes
This is a variation on the *Gambling on Grammar* idea, described by Mario Rinvolucri in his book *Grammar Games*. The sub-skill of hypothesising is practised in Stage 2 when the learners are trying to agree on which statements are true and which are lies. If your aim is to practise related language, remind the learners about this at the start of the stage.

Variations
- **Organised Chaos Variation** – In Stage 1, instead of asking one question at a time, the two teams 'mingle', with several different conversations happening simultaneously for a specified time period. Anybody can ask a question to anybody else during this time period, which will take about five minutes.
- **Specific Grammar Point Variation** – If you want to practise a specific grammar point, such as present perfect vs. past simple, *can* for ability or *used to*, you can specify that the learners use only the required structure in their statements.

Lie Auction — Worksheet

Rules of the game

Preparation
Play in teams. Each team completes the 10 statements about their team members in the table below. Five should be lies and five should be true. The statements can be facts, abilities or past events. You can write several statements about each team member if you wish. Then pass the sheet on to another team. Don't complete any of the other columns.

How to play

Stage 1
The two teams should sit together. Each team has exactly five minutes to ask the other team about their statements in order to decide which ones are lies.

Stage 2
Your team should guess which of the other team's statements are true and which are lies. Write 'truth' or 'lie' in the box. Next choose a sum to bet. You can gamble between $100 and $1000 on each statement. Write the sum in the box 'Bet'.

Stage 3
The two teams reveal which statements are lies, and then each team works out how much money it has made or lost in total.

How to win
The team that makes the most money wins!

Team Name: _____

Complete the table with 10 statements about your team members. Five should be true and five should be lies.

Statement	Truth or lie?	Bet	Profit or loss
E.g. Marco has won a prize for his Tango dancing.			
1			
2			
3			
4			
5			
6			
7			
8			
9			
10			
		Total profit:	

© Delta Publishing 2014 — SPEAKING GAMES by Jason Anderson

Word Countdown

Time	20–30 minutes
Interaction	Whole class divided into 2–6 teams
Level	B1 (Intermediate) to C1 (Advanced)

Language areas practised

Sub-skills and Functions
- manipulating sentence syntax at speed
- connecting ideas creatively

Grammar and Lexis
- sentence formation
- linking expressions
- relative and subordinate clauses
- past tenses

Preparation
Photocopy the **Rules of the game** (one per team) and the **Word cards** from page 125 of the Resource bank (one set for the class). Cut up the Word cards and put them into a bag. Find a timer that you can display easily (e.g. mobile phone). Teams work best with between two and five learners.

Notes
Make sure teams understand the rule that the sentence must be written down. This helps make the game more dynamic and assists with invigilation.

Variations
- **Personalised Variation** – Add a few more cards with the names of some of the learners in the classroom. Choose learners who don't mind being the centre of attention!
- **Dynamic Variation** – Write the words on the Word cards on larger flashcards which can be stuck on the board with Blu-tac™. Give mini white boards and markers to the teams to write their sentences on.
- **Green Variation** – Display the rules on a projector or explain them yourself to reduce paper usage.

Word Countdown — Rules of the game

Preparation
Play as a whole class. Form two to six teams. The class needs a one-minute timer (e.g mobile phone) and a 'word bag'.

How to play
One volunteer comes to the front and takes 10 words from the word bag, which he writes on the board. All the teams now have one minute to write down a sentence that includes as many of these words as possible. The sentence can include any other words, and must be grammatically correct (see example below). Each team reads out their sentence and the scores are calculated. Then the words are put back into the word bag and another round begins.

How to score and win
Each team gets one point for each of the words on the board that are in their sentence. They do not score points for other words not on the board. The scores are kept and the team with the highest score at the end of the game wins.

Example
The following 10 cards were taken from the word bag:

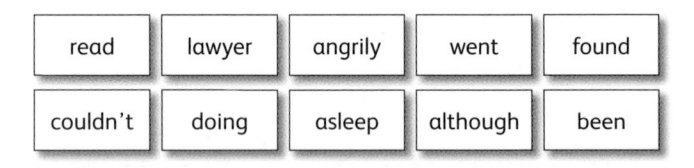

| read | lawyer | angrily | went | found |
| couldn't | doing | asleep | although | been |

The following sentence would score seven points for the cards used (in bold):

Although we found the lawyer asleep, we couldn't understand what he had been doing

If…
- If a team has not finished writing their sentence at the end of a minute, they do not score any points, even if they can say the sentence. It must be written down!
- If a team's sentence is grammatically incorrect, they lose one point for each error. The teacher decides how many errors the sentence contains.

SPEAKING GAMES by Jason Anderson © Delta Publishing 2014

Riddle Race

Time	30–40 minutes
Interaction	Groups of 3–5 learners
Level	B1 (Intermediate) to C1 (Advanced)

Language areas practised

Sub-skills and Functions

- lateral / creative thinking
- explaining an abstract idea

Grammar and Lexis

- conjunctions for explaining and justifying: *because, so, if, but*, etc.

Preparation

Photocopy the **Rules of the game**, the **Solutions sheet** and the **Riddle cards** on page 85 (one of each per group). Cut up the Riddle cards as indicated.

Notes

The aim of this activity is to provide learners with practice in explaining abstract ideas and concepts using lateral thinking. Make sure they explain their answers fully. There are many 'red herrings' on the Solution sheet that will lead learners into providing creative, but incorrect, solutions!

Variations

- Write the 15 correct solutions on the board and give each learner a Riddle card. They mingle with each other, reading out their riddles, guessing the answers from those on the board and providing explanations. They award points to each other if the explanation is correct.

Riddle Race — Rules of the game

Preparation

Play in groups of 3-5. Each group needs a **Solution sheet**, a set of **Riddle cards** and a pen. Place the Solution sheet between the players and the Riddle cards in a pile, face down, in the middle of the Solution sheet.

How to play

Take turns to take a Riddle card and read out the riddle. The answer to the riddle is somewhere on the Solution sheet. The first player to shout out the answer <u>must explain</u> why this is the answer. If her answer and explanation are correct, she writes her name on that square. She now takes the next Riddle card and reads out the riddle. The game continues in this way. Be careful – there are many words on the Solution sheet that are not correct answers!

How to win

The player who has written their name on the most squares at the end of the game is the winner.

If...

- If a player provides an incorrect answer, allow her to finish her solution. Then say 'no' and invite other solutions.
- If a player provides a correct answer, but not the correct reason, that card is moved to the bottom of the pile of Riddle cards and the player can't write her name on the square.
- If two players shout out different solutions at the same time, allow them both to provide explanations before confirming which is correct.
- If two players shout out the same solution at the same time, the player who is losing can provide their explanation first.

Riddle Race

Solution sheet

Section 4: Puzzles & Challenges

water	short	nothing	zero	teapot	Eve
water	short	nothing	zero	teapot	Eve
envelope	coal	a ball	tea	your age	a stamp
envelope	coal	a ball	tea	your age	a stamp
time	love		a cold	teapot
time	love	PLACE THE RIDDLE CARDS HERE	a cold	teapot
Ena	a promise		nineteen	Mary
Ena	a promise		nineteen	Mary
fourteen	money	rain	Edam	a clock	silence
fourteen	money	rain	Edam	a clock	silence
Cheddar	a year	the moon	prices	the sun	a towel
Cheddar	a year	the moon	prices	the sun	a towel

SPEAKING GAMES by Jason Anderson © Delta Publishing 2014

Riddle Race — Riddle cards

Section 1: Board Games

What can you catch but not throw?

a cold

In English you can say *'catch'* a cold to mean *'get the infection from someone'*. The opposite is *'give a cold'*.

Which word becomes shorter when you add two letters to it?

short

If you add the two letters *'er'* to the end of the word *'short'* you get the comparative *'shorter'*.

What gets wetter as it dries?

a towel

As a towel dries your hands, it becomes wetter itself.

The poor have it, the rich need it and if you eat it you'll die. What is it?

nothing

The poor have nothing, the rich need nothing and if you eat nothing you'll starve.

What begins in *'e'*, ends in *'e'* but may have only one letter in it?

envelope

The word *'envelope'* begins and ends with the letter *'e'*, and may only contain one letter.

What cheese is made backwards?

Edam

If you reverse the order of the letters in the word *'made'*, you get the word *'Edam'*, a cheese from Holland.

What can travel around the world but stay in the same corner?

a stamp

A stamp travels on a letter, but always stays in the top right corner of the letter.

What goes up, but never comes down?

your age

'Go up' can also mean *'increase'*, and your age can increase but never decrease.

What's black when you buy it, red when you use it and white when you've finished with it?

coal

Coal is black when you buy it, red when it's burning, and the ashes are white when it's used.

What begins in *'t'*, ends in *'t'* and has only *'t'* in it?

teapot

The word *'teapot'* starts and finishes with the letter *'t'*. Inside a teapot, you find the drink *'tea'*.

How many letters aren't in the alphabet?

nineteen

The two words *'the alphabet'* contain 7 letters: *t, h, e, a, l, p, b*. If we subtract these from the 26 letters of the alphabet we get 19.

It's been around for billions of years, but never grows older than a month. What is it?

the moon

Each cycle of the moon only takes one month, but the moon itself is much older.

What has a face and hands but no arms or legs?

a clock

In English (and other languages), the pointers on a clock are called *'hands'*, and the round flat part is called the *'face'*.

If you say its name you will break it. What is it?

silence

If you say the word *'silence'* you will be 'breaking the silence', which is a common collocation in English.

Mary's father has five daughters, Ana, Bana, Cana, and Dana are four. Who is the fifth?

Mary

We know that Mary is one of the daughters, and the other four have been named.

© Delta Publishing 2014 — SPEAKING GAMES by Jason Anderson

400;# Who wants to be an 'Idiom'aire?

Time	15–40 minutes
Interaction	Teams of 2–4 learners
Level	B1 (Intermediate) to C1 (Advanced)

Language areas practised

Sub-skills and Functions

- predicting the meaning of unfamiliar lexis
- providing reasons for choices
- coming to an agreement

Grammar and Lexis

- idioms

Preparation

Photocopy the **Rules of the game**, the **Game board** and the answers (one of each between teams). Each team will need a counter and a one-minute stopwatch (e.g. mobile phone). They will also need a few paper dictionaries or access to online/electronic dictionaries. Distribute the correct answers to each team and tell them to keep these secret from their opponents.

Notes

This game encourages learners to guess the meaning of idioms, provoking a lot of natural discussion and coming to agreement within teams as they evaluate the three options. The idioms at the bottom of the board are some of the most commonly used 'guessable' idioms in English. They get progressively more difficult as the players move up the board.

Variations

- **Higher Levels** – Learners can play in pairs rather than teams.
- **Lower Levels** – They can use each Lifeline twice.

Who wants to be an 'Idiom'aire? — Rules of the game

Preparation

Play in teams of 2-4 players against a different team. Each team will need a counter and the answers for the other team's questions. You'll need a one-minute timer (e.g. mobile phone) for the 'Use a Dictionary' lifeline.

How to play

Team A goes first, moving their counter forward one space. Read the idiom and the example sentence and then choose the answer, a), b) or c) that best defines the idiom. If the team is not sure of the answer they can get some help (see 'Lifelines'). Team B checks the answer. If Team A are right, they move forward to the next square (but wait for their next turn to guess the idiom). If they are wrong, they stay on the same square (and must try to answer the same question again on their next turn). Team B plays next. Note the following:

- You must get an answer right before you can move forward, so you might need to try the same question three times.
- You don't lose if you get an answer wrong, you just stay where you are.

How to win

The first team to reach $1,000,000 wins the game!

Lifelines

You can use any of your three lifelines at any time during the game. Once you have used a lifeline, cross it out. You can't use it again.

- **Ask the teacher** – Your teacher will give you a clear example context for how to use the idiom.
- **Use a dictionary** – You have exactly one minute to try to find the answer using a dictionary.
- **50/50** – The other team will remove one of the incorrect options, leaving only the correct option and one incorrect option. They can choose which one to leave.

Answers - Team B
Here are the answers to Team A's questions.
Don't let team A see them!:
1.a 2.c 3.b 4.a 5.b 6.a 7.c 8.b 9.a 10.a

Answers - Team A
Here are the answers to Team B's questions.
Don't let team B see them!:
1.a 2.b 3.a 4.c 5.b 6.b 7.b 8.b 9.a 10.a

SPEAKING GAMES by Jason Anderson © Delta Publishing 2014

Who wants to be an 'Idiom'aire?   Game board

$1,000,000

Team A		Team B
10. a chip on one's shoulder *'She's definitely got a chip on her shoulder.'* a) an ability to take offence easily b) a natural skill for cooking c) strong ambition	**$500,000**	**10. go cold turkey** *'He's decided to go cold turkey.'* a) rehabilitate one's self from drugs or alcohol b) betray someone you love to the police c) leave home as a teenager or young adult
9. against the grain *'I think his decision goes against the grain.'* a) different to what is normal or natural b) risky c) ignoring the feelings of others	**$250,000**	**9. kick the bucket** *'I heard Frank's finally kicked the bucket.'* a) die b) resign from a long-term job c) retire
8. go Dutch *'Let's go Dutch on this one.'* a) agree to disagree in a discussion or debate b) split a restaurant bill equally c) go by bicycle	**$125,000**	**8. the last straw** *'That was the last straw!'* a) a deadline or important date b) the final, unacceptable problem or mistake c) the end of a supply of something important
7. pull someone's leg *'Are you pulling my leg?'* a) invite somebody on a date b) accuse someone of being bad at sport c) tease someone in a joke	**$64,000**	**7. below the belt** *'That comment was below the belt.'* a) lacking intelligence or knowledge b) unkind or cruel c) inappropriately sexual
6. a hot potato *'Yes, that topic's a real hot potato at the moment.'* a) a complex topic that often divides opinion b) a topic that everyone is tired of discussing c) a topic of interest among the working class only	**$32,000**	**6. paint the town red** *'I'm painting the town red tonight.'* a) stay in and work or study b) go out and have lots of fun c) experience the famous sights of a town
5. tie the knot *'They've finally decided to tie the knot.'* a) inform their families about a secret relationship b) get married c) move in together as a couple	**$16,000**	**5. over the hill** *'He's over the hill, I'm afraid.'* a) too boring b) too old c) too different from one's partner / spouse
4. over the moon *'I was over the moon when I heard the news.'* a) very happy b) very angry c) unsure how to react	**$8,000**	**4. hit the nail on the head** *'Actually, I think Mark's hit the nail on the head.'* a) behave too aggressively b) finish a project or task early c) describe a situation or solution accurately
3. bite off more than one can chew *'She's bitten off more than she can chew this time.'* a) spend more money than one can pay back b) take on a project or job that is too difficult c) pretend to be an expert	**$4,000**	**3. cost (someone) an arm and a leg** *'His new car cost him an arm and a leg.'* a) cost a lot b) included a hidden cost c) caused a serious accident
2. a piece of cake *'That exam was a piece of cake, wasn't it?'* a) part of a larger problem b) very enjoyable c) very easy	**$2,000**	**2. lend (someone) a hand** *'Could you lend us a hand, please?'* a) sign a document b) help c) provide help with counting up to fifteen
1. keep an eye on something *'Could you keep an eye on my bag, please?'* a) watch something b) rest your head on something c) take a photo of something	**$1,000**	**1. break somebody's heart** *'You've broken his heart!'* a) hurt the feelings of someone who loves you b) feed someone too much high fat food c) kill someone in a fight
TEAM A START	**$0**	**TEAM B START**

Team A Lifelines: ASK THE TEACHER / USE A DICTIONARY / 50/50

Team B Lifelines: ASK THE TEACHER / USE A DICTIONARY / 50/50

Section 4: Puzzles & Challenges

Section 4: Puzzles & Challenges

How to Rob a Bank

Time	40–60 minutes
Interaction	Teams of 3–5 learners
Level	B1 (Intermediate) to C1 (Advanced)

Language areas practised

Sub-skills and Functions

- describing sequences of events
- making suggestions
- justifying ideas and opinions

Grammar and Lexis

- modal verbs of possibility
- 1st and 2nd conditional structures
- crime and courtroom

Preparation

Photocopy the **Instructions** and the **Plan of the Bank** (one of each per team). Allow 10–20 minutes preparation time for each team to plan their presentation.

If possible, arrange a way of projecting the Plan of the bank onto the board or a wall for the presentation stage. This could be done using an interactive whiteboard or data projector (scan the plan into a PC or photograph and transfer) or an Overhead Projector (copy the plan onto an OHP transparency). This makes the presentations more interesting and replicates the mood of a 'heist meeting'. After the presentations, mix up the teams to discuss the different plans and to decide as a group which is best. This leads to more discussion, debate and justification of opinions.

Notes

This controversial topic has been chosen as it's a familiar theme of many Hollywood movies and computer games. It should be introduced as a game: *'Imagine you are in a movie or playing a computer game'*. It may not be appropriate for all classes. Nonetheless, in classes where it is appropriate, it generates considerable discussion and debate, challenging learners to offer suggestions, provide reasons for their opinions and describe sequences of events in careful detail.

Variations

- In small classes (up to eight learners), they can work as a whole class team for a shorter speaking activity.

How to Rob a Bank   Instructions

Preparation

Play in teams of 3-5 learners. You are professional bank robbers. Your teacher will give you the secret plans to the WFM Bank in Bridgetown. Choose a name for your team.

How to play

Stage 1

In your team discuss and agree on the best method for robbing the bank.

Stage 2

Each team presents their method to the class.

Stage 3

The class decides on the best method.

Presentations

During your presentation, you must answer the following questions:

1) What items will you need? How will you get them?
2) How will you rob the bank?
3) What possible problems do you predict? How will you deal with them?

Notes

- You have a budget of $5,000 only.
- You can't use guns or violence.
- Bank opening times are 9am to 5pm, Monday to Saturday. It's busiest at lunchtimes and on Saturday mornings.
- The bank is unmanned at night, but the alarms are switched on. If they are set off, the alarms will call the police (three minutes response time).

SPEAKING GAMES by Jason Anderson   © Delta Publishing 2014

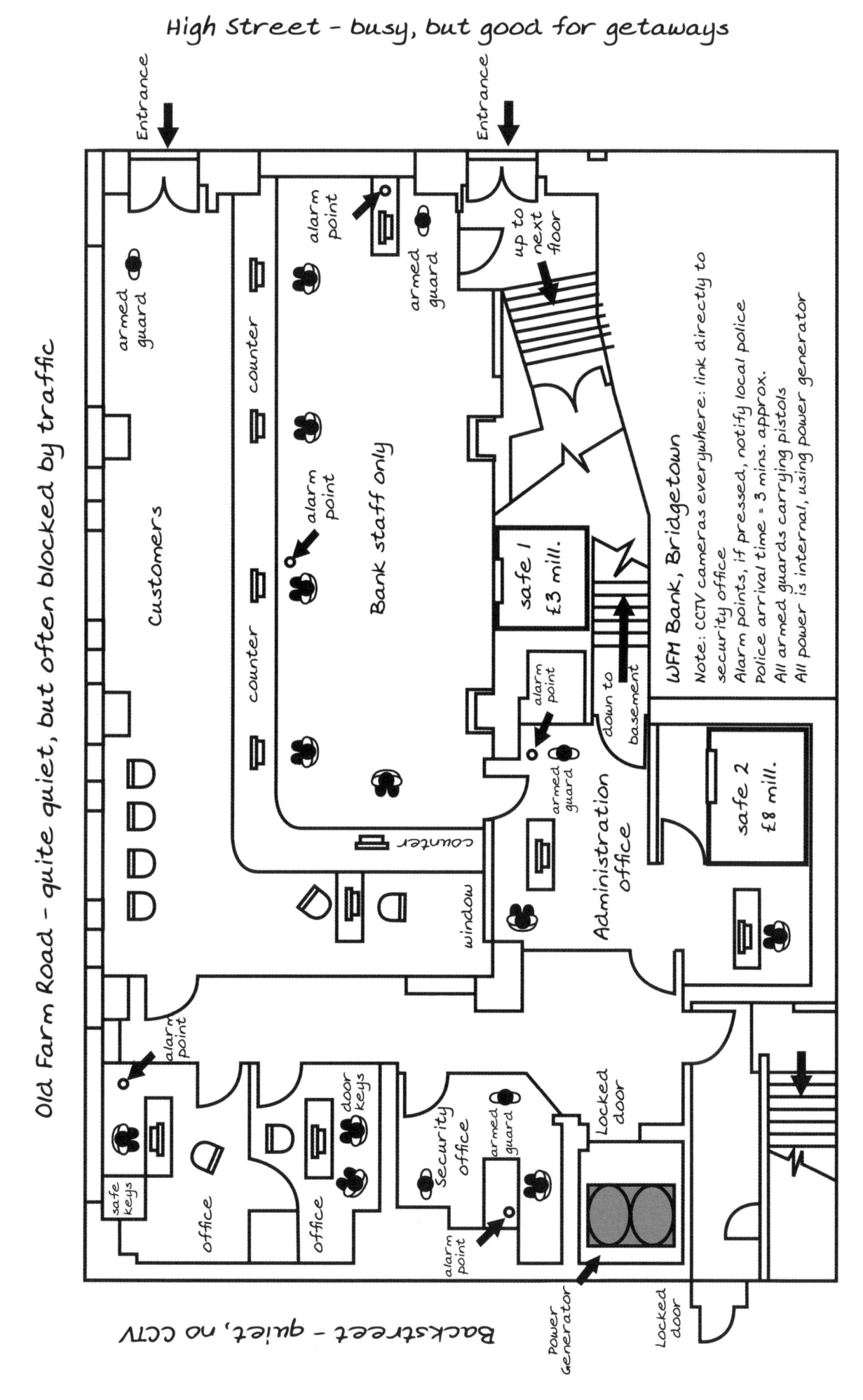

How to Rob a Bank

Plan of the bank

Section 4: Puzzles & Challenges

High Street – busy, but good for getaways

Entrance ↓   Entrance ↓

- armed guard
- alarm point
- armed guard
- up to next floor
- counter
- alarm point
- counter
- Customers
- Bank staff only
- counter
- window
- alarm point
- armed guard
- Administration office
- safe 1 – £3 mill.
- down to basement
- safe 2 – £8 mill.

WFM Bank, Bridgetown

Note: CCTV cameras everywhere: link directly to security office.
Alarm points, if pressed, notify local police.
Police arrival time = 3 mins. approx.
All armed guards carrying pistols.
All power is internal, using power generator.

- safe keys
- office
- door keys
- office
- alarm point
- Security office
- armed guard
- Locked door
- alarm point
- Power Generator
- Locked door

Old Farm Road – quite quiet, but often blocked by traffic

Backstreet – quiet, no CCTV

© Delta Publishing 2014   SPEAKING GAMES by Jason Anderson   89

The Key to the Problem

Time	20–35 minutes
Interaction	Groups of 3–4 learners
Level	B1 (Intermediate) to C1 (Advanced)

Language areas practised

Sub-skills and Functions

- describing procedures in detail
- describing diagrams or movements
- making presentations
- justifying a suggestion

Grammar and Lexis

- verbs of movement and action
- tools

Preparation

Photocopy the **Worksheet** (one copy per group). Groups may also need paper and pens to draw diagrams to help communicate their solutions. If they have flip chart paper and marker pens, the diagrams can also be used in the presentations.

Notes

Encourage groups to make their presentations together rather than just one or two members presenting. Occasionally a group (or an individual within the group) may decide upon a solution quickly, presume it's the best one and stop discussing. If so, encourage them to think of a second solution in case it's an improvement on the first one.

Variations

- **Silent Preparation Variation** – Before they work in their groups, give each learner 2–3 minutes to work individually and make notes. This is likely to encourage more discussion and more accurate and varied use of language. It's also a good idea at lower levels.
- **Democratic Variation** – Learners decide on the best solution, but aren't allowed to vote for their own group. This variation needs three groups or more to work.
- **Complex Scoring Variation** – Award marks not just for the solution that is most likely to work, but also for best presentation, clearest diagrams, willingness to accept criticism, etc.

The Key to the Problem

Worksheet

Preparation
Work in groups of 3-4. Discuss the problem below for 10 minutes. Each group will then present their solution to the class. Your teacher and classmates will listen and ask questions if necessary during the presentations.

The Problem
You were walking home when you dropped your key down a hole. The hole is too narrow and dangerous to climb down. Luckily, your house is nearby and you left your garden shed open. Inside the shed are all the things you see in the picture below. You can use <u>only</u> these items in your solution. Feel free to draw diagrams and images that you can use in your presentations.

How to win
Your teacher will choose the solution that s/he thinks is most likely to succeed in getting the key out.

If…
- If an aspect of a solution is not clear to your teacher or classmates, they can ask questions. They may also offer criticisms or concerns for you to respond to. Feel free to use the board or gesture to make your solution clear.

Section 4: Puzzles & Challenges

© Delta Publishing 2014

SPEAKING GAMES by Jason Anderson

91

Third Person Challenge

Time	15–25 minutes
Interaction	Pairs
Level	B1 (Intermediate) to B2 (Upper Intermediate)

Language areas practised

Sub-skills and Functions

- Accurately manipulating form when responding to questions

Grammar and Lexis

- Present simple tense, 3rd person

Preparation

Photocopy the **Rules of the game** and the two **Question sheets** (one of each per pair).

Notes

If your learners are forgetting to use the 3rd person 's', this game is for you! It has been designed to do two things:

- ensure learners continue to pay attention to this area of grammar while communicating under time pressure
- get learners to provide instant correction of each other's mistakes with 3rd person 's'.

Delayed correction is unlikely to be of use with this type of grammar 'slip'. Learners know the rule, but just forget to use it!

After playing this game, you can encourage them to continue peer-correcting this easy-to-spot error.

Variations

- Learners can improvise their own questions.
- Learners can see how many questions they can answer in one minute without making a mistake.
- Put one learner in the 'hot seat' at the end of each lesson. Classmates all prepare one 3rd person question each, and the learner in the hot seat tries to answer them all correctly.

Third Person Challenge — Rules of the game

Preparation
Play in pairs. Your teacher will give you both a **Question sheet**:
- Learner A: Pick up your Question sheet.
- Learner B: Don't look at yours yet. Keep it on the desk, face down.

Each pair also needs a timer (e.g. mobile phone).

How to play
Learner A, get your timer ready. Learner B will have three minutes to answer all the questions on your Question sheet, <u>speaking only</u>. Learner B must:
- answer all of the questions using complete sentences
- use present simple tense only
- never forget to use the 's' on the 3rd person verb, positive or negative!

Don't show the questions and don't take any notes. When you finish, swap over so Learner B asks the questions on his question sheet.

If…
- If your partner doesn't understand the question, repeat it a little more slowly.
- If your partner doesn't use a full sentence answer, say: *'Full sentence, please!'*
- If your partner forgets to use the 3rd person 's', correct him instantly!

How to win
The learner who makes the fewest mistakes wins!

Third Person Challenge — Question sheets

Learner A – Question sheet
Start the timer – 3 minutes only!

1. Where does your best friend live?
2. Where does he/she work?
3. How long does a minute last?
4. What does your pen do?
5. What does your father watch on TV?
6. What about your mother?
7. What does a tiger eat?
8. Who sings the best in your family?
9. What does the sun do?
10. What does a baby do when it's sad?
11. What else does it do?
12. How many languages does a fish speak?

Learner B – Question sheet
Start the timer – 3 minutes only!

1. What does a teacher do every day?
2. What about at night?
3. What happens to a fish in a desert?
4. Who cooks the best in your family?
5. And who eats the most?
6. What time does this lesson end?
7. Where does a monkey live?
8. Who talks the most in this class?
9. Who doesn't talk enough?
10. What does a smoker do with cigarettes?
11. Does he speak better English than you? (point at someone in the room)
12. How well does an elephant dance?

© Delta Publishing 2014 — SPEAKING GAMES by Jason Anderson

Be Reasonable

Time	20–40 minutes
Interaction	Groups of 2–5 learners
Level	B1 (Intermediate) to C1 (Advanced)

Language areas practised

Sub-skills and Functions

- providing reasons
- disputing and justifying opinions
- describing hypothetical situations

Grammar and Lexis

- linkers of reason and purpose (*because, in order to, so that*, etc.)
- *would, could* and *should* to describe hypothetical situations

Preparation

Photocopy the **Rules of the game** (one copy per team) and the **Reason cards** from page 120 of the Resource bank (2-4 per team). The number of Reason cards needed will depend on how long you want the game to last. The game works best with 3-5 teams. The preparation stage will take from 6-12 minutes depending on the number of cards each team gets. You'll also need a one-minute timer (e.g. mobile phone). It's a good idea to start with a teacher-demonstrated example. Choose one of the cards that you won't need or use the following: *'Reasons for failing an exam'*.

Notes

As well as the obvious speaking practice this game provides, it also aims to generate debate on the validity of reasons in order to promote more ambitious language use. It's also useful for developing critical, creative and analytical thinking skills. Keep score carefully.

Variations

- Use the Pros and Cons cards from the Resource bank (page 119) rather than the Reason cards.

Be Reasonable

Rules of the game

Preparation

Play in teams of 2-5 players. Each team will need several **Reason cards** and should complete each card with as many reasons as possible in note form (continue on the back if necessary). Spend about three minutes on each card.

How to play

Team A chooses one of their cards and reads out the heading. The other teams have one minute to note down as many reasons they can think of. After one minute, the other teams take turns to give reasons. If the reason is on Team A's card, they score one point. If the reason is relevant, but not on Team A's card, they score two points. After the other teams have given all the reasons they have, Team A read out any reasons that the other teams did not mention, and score one point for each of these reasons. Team B goes next.

How to win

The team with the highest score at the end of the game wins.

If...

- If you mention a reason already provided by another team, you score no points and must wait till the next round to provide your next reason.
- If teams disagree about whether a reason is relevant, consult your teacher. His decision is final.
- If the other teams guess all the reasons on your card, they score one bonus point each.

Needs Analysis Challenge

Time	40–60 minutes
Interaction	Groups of 3–4 learners
Level	B1 (Intermediate) to C1 (Advanced)

Language areas practised

Sub-skills and Functions
- describing needs, preferences and interests
- discussing and coming to a consensus
- expressing opinions

Grammar and Lexis
- education
- language learning

Preparation
Photocopy the **Rules of the game**, the **Game board** and the **Feedback cards** on page 97 (one of each per group). Cut up the cards as indicated. Groups also need dice and counters (e.g. coins) to play.

Notes
This game aims to turn needs analysis into a social event. It provides an opportunity for learners to learn about each other's needs, interests and learning preferences, thereby laying the foundations for good participatory learning through mutual understanding. It's useful to do this in any class, but especially when learners have diverse needs and interests and would benefit from being more aware of the teacher's need to balance between these. It could also be used during a tutorial lesson with learners playing in groups while the teacher interviews learners individually. There is no real need for anyone to win, but in case your class enjoys the competition, this has been included in the rules!

Variations
- **More Discussion** – When a player lands on a question, every player in the group answers it.
- **More Feedback** – The whole group discussion is recorded by one of the players (e.g. on a mobile phone) and the recording is given to the teacher afterwards.
- **Reflection on Learning** – Learners write a short text on what they learnt about their classmates for homework.

Needs Analysis Challenge

Rules of the game

Preparation
Play in groups of 3-4. Each group needs a **Game board**, a dice and a set of **Feedback cards**. Shuffle the cards and place them in a pile, face down, next to the game board. Each player needs a counter (e.g. coins): put them on the **Start square**.

How to play
Take turns to roll the dice and choose which direction to move in. If you land on a square with a question, you must answer the question. If you land on a **Feedback square**, you must take a Feedback card and complete it (see below). Player B rolls next.

Feedback cards
The player who lands on a Feedback square must take and complete a Feedback card by discussing the question with the whole group and summarising the discussion in note form. You can continue on the back if necessary. Try to agree before completing it. Cross out the square on the board.

How to win
The game finishes when all the Feedback cards have been completed. The player who has completed the most is the winner. When you've finished, give the feedback cards to your teacher, who can use them to plan future lessons.

If...
- If a Feedback square has already been crossed out, other players can't land on it. Move to the next available square.

Needs Analysis Challenge — Game board

Section 4: Puzzles & Challenges

	What were your first experiences of learning English like?	How important is error correction in language learning?		How do you hope your English will improve over the next year?	What activities do you find helpful when you are learning new grammar?	
What do you think are your weakest skills? Why?			What kind of activities do you learn most from?			What techniques do you find useful for learning vocabulary?
Can classmates help each other to learn? Give reasons for your answer.			Why are you learning English?			Why do you think some people are more successful at learning languages than others?
	What do you find most difficult about learning English?	What kind of activities do you enjoy doing in class?	**START**	What do you currently use English for?	What is the role of the teacher in language learning?	
What is the best way for learners to learn new vocabulary quickly?			What area of your English would you most like to improve?			Describe a really useful lesson that you remember in the past.
Think of 3 things that a successful language learner does every day.			Which skill do you least enjoy practising in class? Why?			Some people are social learners, others are private learners. What about you?
	What is the biggest difference between the grammar of English and your language?	Who was your favourite teacher at school and why?		Have you ever taken any exams in English? Was it a positive experience?	'Making mistakes is an important part of language learning.' Do you agree?	

SPEAKING GAMES by Jason Anderson © Delta Publishing 2014

Needs Analysis Challenge — Feedback cards

Section 4: Puzzles & Challenges

Discuss as a Group. Summarise the discussion below:

What help do we want with error correction:

a) from the teacher?

b) from each other?

Discuss as a Group. Summarise the discussion below:

What reasons for learning English do we share?

Discuss as a Group. Summarise the discussion below:

What makes a good teacher? Think of five ideas:

1)

2)

3)

4)

5)

Discuss as a Group. Summarise the discussion below:

What activities do we all enjoy doing?
Try to list at least five:

Discuss as a Group. Summarise the discussion below:

What interests and hobbies do we share?

Discuss as a Group. Summarise the discussion below:

Which of the four skills (speaking, writing, reading, listening) are most important for us to practise in class? 1 is most important; 4 is least important:

1)

2)

3)

4)

Now write a percentage (%) next to each skill to indicate how much time should be spent on it. The total should make 100%.

Discuss as a Group. Summarise the discussion below:

What kind of homework do we find useful, and how much should we receive each lesson?

Discuss as a Group. Summarise the discussion below:

What online learning activities do we enjoy doing?

© Delta Publishing 2014 — SPEAKING GAMES by Jason Anderson

Dopey Dave

Time	15–30 minutes
Interaction	Pairs
Level	B1 (Intermediate) to C1 (Advanced)

Language areas practised

Sub-skills and Functions
- telling a story
- describing events in detail

Grammar and Lexis
- narrative tenses
- time expressions
- shopping
- relationships

Preparation

Photocopy the **Comic strip** of the story and the **Player A and Player B Worksheets** (one of each per pair). Cut up as indicated. In class, hand out first the Worksheets to the relevant players and then the Comic strip. Give them time to read the instructions and check that everybody understands that they have different 'scoring words' to their partner on their Worksheet. Make sure they don't show their Worksheet to their partner. Give them three minutes to prepare for telling the story, allowing dictionaries and other resources. Stress the importance of making simple 'bullet point' notes, rather than writing sentences. Player A tells the story first, so player B's words are a little easier.

Notes

Preparation for speaking tasks is known to improve both accuracy and fluency. This game adds an element of complexity (range of vocabulary) by encouraging them to use as wide a vocabulary range as possible. An optional writing task could follow (e.g. for homework), in which the learners tell the story from either Dave's or Tina's perspective. Any similarity to people called Dave, either alive or dead, is purely coincidental!

Variations

- **Lower levels** – Learners have five minutes to prepare.
- **Teamwork** – Learners tell the story in two-player teams, practising in pairs beforehand.
- **Higher levels** – Learners add more words to their 'points boxes' for their partner to score.

Dopey Dave
Player A Worksheet

Preparation
You and your partner are going to tell the same story. Look at the images and make notes for 2–3 minutes. You can use a dictionary if you wish.

How to play
First you will tell your partner the story. Your partner has a list of words and will award you points if you use any of these words, so tell the story in as much detail as you can!

Your partner will then tell the same story. Listen and give him/her points if s/he uses any of the words in your table. Note the words in your table are different to the words in your partner's table.

How to win
The player who scores the most points wins.

Give 1 point for each of these words:	Give 2 points for each of these words:	Give 3 points for each of these words:
shopping	shirt	bump into
bottle	ask	spill
walk	push	aisle
bag	car park	clumsy
restaurant	propose	unfortunately
ring	mad	blame

Dopey Dave
Player B Worksheet

Preparation
You and your partner are going to tell the same story. Look at the images and make notes for 2–3 minutes. You can use a dictionary if you wish.

How to play
First your partner will tell you the story. Listen and give him/her points if s/he uses any of the words in the table below.

Then you tell the same story. Your partner has different words to you and will give points if you use those words.

How to win
The player who scores the most points wins.

Give 1 point for each of these words:	Give 2 points for each of these words:	Give 3 points for each of these words:
supermarket	dress	drop
trolley	invite	soak
wine	car boot / trunk	apologise
say	carry	careless
car	marry	surprisingly
dinner	angry	fault

Section 4: Puzzles & Challenges

© Delta Publishing 2014 — SPEAKING GAMES by Jason Anderson

Dopey Dave — Comic Strip

Section 4: Puzzles & Challenges

THE ADVENTURES OF DOPEY DAVE

(DAVE) ... (TINA) ...

FINISH THE STORY

Short Answer Challenge

Time	10–15 minutes
Interaction	Pairs
Level	B1 (Intermediate) to B2 (Upper Intermediate)

Language areas practised

Sub-skills and Functions

- asking *yes / no* questions
- eliciting a chosen answer to a question
- providing short answers to questions

Grammar and Lexis

- auxiliary verbs including modal auxiliaries
- *yes / no* questions
- short answers

Preparation

Photocopy **Player A** and **Player B Worksheets** (one set per pair). If necessary, do an example on the board before they begin. For example, if the answer required is: *'Yes, I have.'*, the learner could ask: *'Have you cleaned your teeth today?'* Remind learners to answer their partner's questions honestly. They will need a timer (e.g. mobile phone) to time their partner.

Notes

This challenge provides structured practice using auxiliary verbs – both in questions and answers – within a creative framework that encourages honest responses.

Variations

- Instead of working in pairs, learners mingle around the classroom with their Worksheet. They can only ask one question to each person they meet and then must move on (they can come back to the same person later). The first learner to tick all their answers wins!

Short Answer Challenge — Player A Worksheet

1) You have five minutes. You must ask your partner questions to get the following answers:

- ☐ Yes, I have.
- ☐ No, we didn't.
- ☐ No, I can't.
- ☐ No, they aren't.
- ☐ Yes, you do.
- ☐ No, he won't.
- ☐ Yes, it will.
- ☐ Yes, there are.

2) Player B will now try to do the same. Answer his/her questions honestly.

Short Answer Challenge — Player B Worksheet

1) Player A will ask you some questions for five minutes. Answer them honestly.

2) You have five minutes. You must ask your partner questions to get the following answers:

- ☐ No, I haven't.
- ☐ Yes, we do.
- ☐ Yes, we can.
- ☐ Yes, he should.
- ☐ Yes, they are.
- ☐ No, you don't.
- ☐ No, it won't.
- ☐ Yes, there were.

Crime Scene Investigation

Time	20–30 minutes
Interaction	Pairs
Level	B1 (Intermediate) to C1 (Advanced)

Language areas practised

Sub-skills and Functions
- describing an image in detail
- making inferences
- speculating about past events

Grammar and Lexis
- present continuous
- *There is/are*
- present and past modals of probability
- clothing
- past simple and continuous (see Variations)

Preparation

Photocopy the **Rules of the game** and the **Before** and **After images** of the crime scene (one of each per pair). Give out the Rules first. Before you give out the images, stress the importance of not showing them to their partner.

Notes

This is a variation on the *'Spot the Difference'* information gap activity. Note that there are lots of differences between the two pictures. Remind the learners that their aim is to find the significant differences that indicate a potential suspect. If no pair has identified the correct suspects after 12-15 minutes, allow them to show their pictures to each other and continue discussing and speculating.

The solution

The two robbers are the woman with the pushchair and the street cleaner. Clues include: the violin case (containing the shotgun which is in the cleaner's trolley before and in her pushchair afterwards); the bulging cleaner's refuge sacks (full of cash) after the robbery; the word 'clening' is spelt wrongly on the cleaner's trolley. The woman left the child in the pushchair in the entrance porch to the bank while they committed the robbery!

Variations

- **Past Continuous and Past Simple Practice** – Learners work in pairs. Give them the 'Before' picture. They have three minutes to look at it and describe it using past simple and continuous. Then take it away and give them the 'After' picture. They discuss the differences, e.g. *'He wasn't carrying a bag in the other picture.'*, *'I don't think she had a violin case before the robbery.'* The objective is still the same. They may need to see the 'Before' picture again. If so, take away the 'After' one first!

Crime Scene Investigation

Rules of the game

Preparation

Play in pairs. Sit facing your partner. Your teacher will give each of you a picture. Do not show it to your partner. The two pictures are different.

Your challenge

You are police detectives. Earlier today, two criminals robbed £15,000 in cash from a bank in central London wearing balaclavas and carrying a shotgun. Then… they vanished! Your two images show CCTV footage of the bank just before and just after the robbery (5 minutes apart). There are many differences between the two scenes, but you must find any important differences that identify the two criminals without showing your picture to your partner. You must describe the images in detail to find the differences and use your detective skills to decide which are important! When you think you have found the two suspects, tell your teacher who you think did it and explain how they did it.

How to win

The first team to identify the correct criminals and explain how they did the robbery and vanished, wins the game!

Crime Scene Investigation

The crime scene

Before: 10.25am

After: 10.30am

Section 4: Puzzles & Challenges

Guess the Question

Time	30–40 minutes
Interaction	Groups of 4–7 learners
Level	B1 (Intermediate) to B2 (Upper Intermediate)

Language areas practised

Sub-skills and Functions

- making predictions
- giving personal information

Grammar and Lexis

- question forms
- personal interests

Preparation

Photocopy the **Worksheet** (one for each learner). Cut off the corner labelled **Answer sheet** as indicated and keep it hidden from the learners. Give out the rest of the Worksheet (including the **Question starts**) to each learner and allow time to read the instructions. Check understanding before they begin using the following instruction check questions:

- *In Stage 1, who do you talk to? Can you talk to them in Stages 2 and 3?*
- *What do you tell your partner? Can you write it down? Why is it important to remember what they say?*
- *Who will interview you in Stage 3? Who will they interview you about? How will they mark your answers?*

Notes

This game is a good icebreaker for the start of a course. It encourages learners to share as much personal information as possible (and to listen to each other). The best group size is four (two pairs) or six (three pairs). If you have an extra student, create a 'pair of three', with A remembering B's answers, B remembering C's answers, and C remembering A's answers.

In Stage 1, make sure that the pairs predict and answer as many questions as possible without taking any notes.

For Stage 2, separate the pairs and give each one an Answer sheet so that they can see and answer the questions. Make sure they write their name. One-word answers are fine.

For Stage 3, collect in each learner's answers, reminding them that they still can't communicate with their partner. Sit them in their larger groups of 4-7 and give each learner's answers to a different pair in the group so that they can interview each other about their partner and check the answers. Remind them to reformulate the questions appropriately, e.g. 'What is ~~your~~ Ana's favourite food?' They should keep note of the points scored by the other team during Stage 3.

Guess the Question

Worksheet

Preparation
Play in groups of 4-7. Each player chooses a partner within their group. If necessary, three learners can be partners. The game has three stages.

How to play

Stage 1: Preparation – 10 minutes

Look at the 10 Question starts below. The endings have been removed. In Stage 1, you will try to guess how the question ends and tell your partner your answer. For example, Question 1 starts:

   What's your favourite…

The ending could be *'day?'*, *'colour?'* or *'food?'*. Tell your partner your answer to all these questions, and remember all your partner's answers! You can't write anything down.

Stage 2: Writing – 3 minutes

Sit separately from your partner. Your teacher will give you an Answer sheet with the correct ending to each question. You have three minutes to write your own answers silently. Do not communicate with your partner at this stage. When you have finished, give your Answer sheet to the teacher.

Stage 3: Interviews – 15 minutes

The other learners in your group will interview you about your partner. For every question that you answer correctly, you win one point for you and your partner. They will also interview your partner about you. You can't communicate with your partner at this stage!

How to win
The pair who score the most points in each group wins.

If...
- If your answer does not match the answer that your partner wrote, no point!
- If you try to communicate with your partner in Stages 2 or 3, you lose one point.

Question starts

Try to guess the different possible endings for each question and tell all of your answers to your partner!

1. What's your favourite…
2. What's the name of your closest…
3. Do you live in…
4. Which sports…
5. What colour is your…
6. Which of your parents…
7. At school, what was…
8. Which day of the week…
9. Where did you go for your last…
10. Which famous person…

Answer sheet

Your name: _____

Write your own answers to the questions here:

…food? _____

…friend? _____

…a house or an apartment? _____

…do you find boring? _____

…mobile phone? _____

…do you talk to most? _____

…your best subject? _____

…do you least like? _____

…holiday? _____

…would you most like to marry? _____

What a Coincidence!

Time	30–45 minutes
Interaction	Groups of 2–5 learners
Level	B1 (Intermediate) to C1 (Advanced)

Language areas practised

Sub-skills and Functions
- speculating
- linking ideas together
- formulating a hypothesis
- narrating a story

Grammar and Lexis
- narrative tenses
- past modal verbs of deduction
- time sequencers

Preparation

Photocopy the **Worksheet**, the **Further Information cards** (below) and the **Three stories** from page 122 of the Resource bank (one of each per group). Cut up the Further Information cards as indicated. There is no need to cut up the **Nine clues** on the Worksheet. If possible, get each group to sit closely together. Begin by explaining or checking understanding of *coincidence* and then hand out the Worksheet. Once the learners have read the instructions, ask a few check questions, e.g. *How many stories? How many clues for each story? Why are the stories interesting? What is the aim of the game? How do you score/lose points? How do you lose one point?* Set a clear time frame (20 minutes is about right) and let them begin.

During the game, keep track of how many Further Information cards each team has had. If a team finishes early, get them to write synopses of their three stories. At the end, make sure all teams have completed their answer boxes and then get a few teams to tell the class their own versions of the stories. Provide the correct answers (see the Three Stories in the Resource bank), calculate team scores and hand out the three stories for learners to read.

Notes

The Three stories may be 'urban myths' but all refer to specific people, dates and places. All are widely available on the Internet.

Variations

- **Bonus Points** – If you like, as well as awarding points as described above, you can award bonus points if any team guesses a story exactly.
- **Using Narrative Tenses** – After the learners have read the three stories, get them to retell them to each other from memory. All three include a nice range of narrative tenses.

What a Coincidence — Further Information cards

1. Just as they were waiting for their dinner to arrive, Lara noticed that her wedding ring was missing.

2. She had to send an urgent fax, but the office fax machine had broken down and Sue couldn't repair it.

3. Suddenly, he recognised a person sitting in a wheelchair on the boat.

4. For Christmas, 1999, Mr Stuart Spencer of Sheffield received a jigsaw puzzle as a Christmas present from his daughter.

5. The fish they had ordered was quite big, so Franco cut it in half.

6. She didn't have his telephone number, but luckily she found it on a piece of paper on the office notice board.

7. 'Wait. Sue… I'm not at home. I'm in a telephone box. Where did you get the number?'

8. It showed a picture of an old boat travelling along a canal in Norfolk, a popular holiday spot in England about 200 miles from Mr Spencer's home.

9. That evening, they went to the hotel restaurant and ordered a local fish dish.

SPEAKING GAMES by Jason Anderson © Delta Publishing 2014

What a Coincidence!

Worksheet

Preparation
Play in teams of 2-5 players. Sit together so that other teams can't hear your discussion. The table below shows **9 Clues**. They link to three separate stories about three incredible coincidences. You must decide which three clues belong to each story.

How to play
Begin by discussing the clues. Try to predict the three stories and decide which three clues go with which story. You will need some more information about some of the clues. Your teacher has a **Further Information card** (a sentence from the story) for each clue. You can ask your teacher for any of these cards, but you lose one point from your final score for each Further Information card you take. Begin by asking for the most important ones first, discuss how they fit into the three stories and then decide if you need any more sentences.

How to win
When you think you have worked out the three stories, complete the answer box below. You score five points for guessing the clues in one story correctly and 10 points for guessing the clues in all three stories. But remember that you also lose one point for each Further Information card you take! The team with the most points at the end of the game wins.

Answer box

Story 1 clues: Story 2 clues: Story 3 clues:

What a Coincidence

The Nine Clues

© Delta Publishing 2014

SPEAKING GAMES by Jason Anderson

Section 4: Puzzles & Challenges

107

Guess the Story

Time	25–40 minutes
Interaction	Pairs
Level	B1 (Intermediate) to C1 (Advanced)

Language areas practised

Sub-skills and Functions

- making guesses
- asking questions

Grammar and Lexis

- present continuous
- narrative tenses
- time sequencers

Preparation and Procedure

Photocopy the **Player A** and **Player B Worksheets** (one of each per pair). Tell the learners that they will receive a different story to their partner. Both stories are connected to interesting pictures. The aim of the game is to guess their partner's story. Hand out the two Worksheets, reminding them not to show their sheet to their partner, and let them read their own story. When they've finished reading, point out the facts that their partner must try to guess, reminding them that they can only answer *'Yes'*, *'No'* or *'Maybe'* to their partner's questions. They should take it in turns to ask questions or make guesses. Finally draw their attention to the image at the bottom of their sheet which depicts their partner's story. If necessary, ask a few check questions to make sure they understand the activity, e.g. *'What is the aim of the game?'*, *'How many points can you award?'*, *'What answers can you give to your partner's questions?'* and let them begin. They'll enjoy reading their partner's story when they've finished.

Notes

The *Red Card* story is widely available on the Internet, and the facts and details make it sound credible, if remarkable! The details to *A Crowded Wardrobe* are a bit more sketchy and it may be an urban myth.

Variations

- **Whole Class Variation** – Learners are shown one of the two pictures and they ask you questions to guess the story. You can only answer *'Yes'* or *'No'*.

Guess the Story

Player A Worksheet

Your story – A Crowded Wardrobe

A couple in Holland were woken one night by the sound of a burglar downstairs. They immediately called the local policeman and waited. The local policeman arrived quickly and made enough noise to disturb the burglar, who decided to hide in a large wardrobe. The couple had found a knife and were coming downstairs to try to catch the burglar themselves. The policeman, upon hearing their voices, thought there were two burglars and got scared when he realised he'd forgotten his gun. He found a large wardrobe and decided to hide in it. A few seconds later he realised someone else was in there and screamed. The couple opened the wardrobe door to find the policeman and the burglar together!

Material taken from 'Passeggiate Italiane' by Paola Marmini and Giosi Vicentini (Bonacci editore, Roma).

Player B will ask questions to guess your story. You can only answer 'Yes', 'No' or 'Maybe'. Award one point for each of the following facts:

a) The man next to the police officer is a burglar.

b) The couple opening the wardrobe live in the house.

c) The couple had called the police.

d) The burglar hid in the cupboard when he heard the police arrive.

e) The policeman hid in the cupboard when he heard the couple coming downstairs.

f) The policeman thought the couple were two burglars and got scared.

Here's the picture for Player B's story. You must ask questions and try to guess the facts. Player B will give you points for relevant facts.

Section 4: Puzzles & Challenges

Guess the Story

Player B Worksheet

Your story – Red Card

A Brazilian football referee made an embarrassing mistake during a football match in January 2004. After a dangerous foul, the referee, Carlos Ferro, decided to send a player off by showing him the traditional red card. However, instead of pulling a red card from his pocket, Carlos pulled out a pair of red woman's knickers. Before he realised his mistake, he had lifted the knickers above his head for everyone to see, including his wife who was watching the match. The player asked him if it was a joke, at which moment the referee noticed the knickers in his hand and tried to hide them as quickly as he could. Unfortunately, his wife had seen everything, and was furious with him. His problems increased when she realised that the knickers were not hers. Carlos tried to explain that they were a present for their 16-year-old daughter, but his wife refused to believe him and threw him out of the house. A few days later she filed for divorce.

Player A will ask questions to guess your story. You can only answer 'Yes', 'No' or 'Maybe'.
Award one point for each of the following facts:

a) The player has just fouled another player and received a red card.

b) The referee is holding a pair of women's knickers.

c) The referee didn't realise the knickers were in his pocket.

d) The referee's wife was watching the match.

e) The knickers didn't belong to his wife.

f) The referee's wife divorced him.

Here's the picture for Player A's story. You must ask questions and try to guess the facts. Player A will give you points for relevant facts.

SPEAKING GAMES by Jason Anderson © Delta Publishing 2014

Resource bank

Comparative and Superlative prompt cards

river	car	book	university
place	lake	film	computer
country	word	forest	bird
insect	animal	fish	food
actress	language	leader	mobile phone
company	footballer	game	musician
month	colour	writer	drink
metal	plant	illness	discovery
website	invention	sea	city

Country question cards

Would you like to visit this country? Why (not)?	What languages are spoken in this country?	What's the weather like in this country?
What wild animals live in this country?	What is the capital city of this country?	What would you do if you went on holiday to this country?
What is the food of this country like?	What is this country famous for?	What are the main religions in this country?
What is the landscape like in this country?	What famous products come from this country?	Name a famous person who comes from this country.
What is the most visited tourist attraction in this country?	What is the currency of this country?	What is the national dress of this country like?

Free Time Activity question cards

Have you ever done it? If yes, what did you think of it? If not, why not?	How long ago did people start doing it?	Why do you think people enjoy it?
Where do people usually do it?	How long does it take to do it?	What things do you need to do it?
Do people do it alone or in groups?	Is it more popular among men or women?	What can you learn from doing it?
Is it expensive to do? What are the main costs?	What skills do you need to do it?	What knowledge do you need to do it?
How dangerous is it? What are the risks?	What kind of person does it suit?	Are you planning to do it in the future? If so, when? If not, why not?

Job cards

Opinion cards

'Cars should be banned from city centres.'	'We should be allowed to choose which taxes we contribute to.'	'Global warming has not yet been proven, so I'm not changing my lifestyle.'
'Men make better politicians than women because they are less emotional.'	'Corrupt policemen should, if found guilty, get life imprisonment.'	'Chinese will soon replace English as the first language of the world.'
'Violent films and video games should be banned. They are the cause of a lot of violence in society.'	'Drugs are no worse than alcohol, tobacco, or caffeine.'	'Prisons don't work. They make criminals worse.'
'Boxing should be banned. It's too dangerous.'	'It should be illegal to pay for primary and secondary education.'	'To reduce the world population, it should be illegal for any couple to have more than one child.'
'Advertisements for junk food should be banned, just like advertisements for cigarettes.'	'Women make better leaders because they have more emotional intelligence.'	'The world would be a better place without alcohol.'
'Only soldiers should be allowed to own guns.'	'Very rich people should not have access to public healthcare or education.'	'Schools won't be necessary in 10 years. All learning will happen online.'
'Nuclear energy should be banned in all countries.'	'Restaurants should pay their staff properly so customers don't have to leave tips.'	'Illegal downloading from the Internet is killing the music and film industries.'
'People who want to eat meat should be forced to kill the animals themselves.'	'People are too dependent on computers nowadays.'	'Retirement age should be increased by 10 years.'

Personalisation question cards

| What makes you happy? | How do you intend to use English in the future? | What do you like doing at weekends? |

| What stops you from concentrating? | What dishes do you enjoy preparing? | What makes you lose your temper? |

| What do you want to do after this lesson? | What event in the future are you most looking forward to? | Why did you decide to come to this school? |

| What would you recommend to somebody who wants to lose weight? | What have you given up doing in the last year? | What have you started doing in the last year? |

| What are you thinking of doing for your holidays next year? | What dishes from your country would you suggest trying to a foreign visitor? | What do you hope to do next year? |

| What do you find interesting about learning English? | What are you going to do this weekend? | What helps you to sleep? |

| What are you trying to do to improve your English at the moment? | What do you enjoy doing on your birthday? | What language would you like to learn apart from English? |

Phrasal Verb question cards

What do you usually do on Sunday morning?	get up	What are you doing in your spare time now that you've retired?	take up
Are the two of you going to get married soon?	go out	Are you close to your parents?	get on
What time are you leaving for the airport?	take off	Why are you going to the library?	take out
Do you like to cook your own food?	take away	This bus is very crowded. Do you want to stay on?	get off
Do you still like olives?	go off	Why are you moving to a different flat?	go up
What advice do you have for saving electricity?	turn off	So what did you do when your boyfriend turned up late to your birthday party with no present?	get out
I didn't see the end of the film. Who was the murderer?	turn out	I know I've got a cold, but do you mind if I sit next to you?	go away
So what happened last night when you tried to get into the concert without tickets?	turn away	Why is your new job so difficult?	take on
Can everyone hear the TV OK?	turn up	Did the party finish soon after I left last night?	go on
Did the police catch the bank robbers?	get away	It's very dark in here.	turn on

Pros and Cons cards

advantages of doing sport	disadvantages of being rich and famous	disadvantages of winning the lottery
advantages of being a vegetarian	disadvantages of nuclear power	disadvantages of being a doctor
advantages of living alone	disadvantages of owning a Smartphone	disadvantages of smoking
advantages of not owning a car	advantages of shopping from home	advantages of not washing for a week
advantages of being a good liar	disadvantages of English as the world's international language	disadvantages of having plastic surgery
advantages of losing your mobile phone	disadvantages of supermarkets compared to street markets	advantages of going to prison
advantages of having insomnia	advantages of losing the keys to your home	advantages of doing your homework every day

Reason cards

Reasons for refusing to go on a date	Reasons for complaining in a restaurant	Reasons for pretending to be sick
Reasons for giving up smoking	Reasons for stealing from a supermarket	Reasons for learning a language
Reasons for avoiding air travel	Reasons for having a party	Reasons for not sleeping at night
Reasons for moving house	Reasons for calling the police	Reasons for not washing your hair
Reasons for arguing with your partner	Reasons for buying a dog	Reasons for going to a post office

Regret cards

I bought my brother some sandals, but he already had the same ones.	I went to school on Monday, but it was a public holiday. It was closed.
I ran to the train station to catch my train. But it was delayed by 15 minutes.	I bought some new batteries for my camera. They were the wrong size and didn't work.
I didn't take the exam course my teacher recommended and I failed the exam.	I got married when I was 18, so I didn't travel much when I was young.
I went out last night without a coat and got very wet. I think I've caught a cold! Achoo!	I went out dancing on Tuesday night. On Wednesday I was late for work and lost my job!
I found a wallet with £400 in it and I gave it to the police.	I forgot to lock my car last night, and it was stolen!
I met a really nice guy/girl yesterday. I forgot to ask for his/her phone number!	I left my mobile phone at home this morning and had to go back and get it at lunchtime.
I got a virus on my computer and lost all my documents, photos, everything!	My neighbour had a really loud party last night and I didn't get any sleep.
I had an argument with my boy/girlfriend at the weekend, and s/he left me!	I left my credit card in a shop, so I had to have it cancelled. It's really annoying.

For Mixed Conditionals:

I didn't get a cup of coffee this morning. I'm feeling too tired to learn.	I missed the lesson on conditionals in English. Now I don't understand conditionals!
I started smoking when I was very young and now I'm too unfit to play football.	I studied French at university, but only English is important for my current job.
I let my sister cut my hair and it looks terrible.	I played tennis yesterday and I sprained my wrist. Now I can't write.

Three Stories

Story 1 – The Wedding Ring

The three clues: 1 - ring; 5 - fish; 9 - menu

In May 1977, Franco and Lara Calvino, from Italy, were on holiday with their family on the island of Sardinia. One day, they decided to take a boat trip to the island of Budelli. About 10 minutes before they got to the island, Lara fell off the boat into the sea. Luckily, she was a good swimmer and did not panic. The boat picked her up and they continued with their plans and enjoyed their day together.

That evening, they went to the hotel restaurant and ordered a local fish dish. Just as they were waiting for their dinner to arrive, Lara noticed that her wedding ring was missing. She was very upset and wanted to go and look for it, but then the food arrived. Franco convinced her to stay and eat first. The fish they had ordered was quite big, so Franco cut it in half. As he was cutting through the fish, his knife hit something hard. It was Lara's wedding ring – inside the fish's stomach! They asked the chef and found out that the fish had been caught near the island of Budelli that afternoon. It must have swallowed Lara's lost ring after she had fallen into the sea!

Story 2 – The Telephone Box

The three clues: 2 - fax machine; - 6 - post-it note with number; 7 - telephone box

One July evening in 1992, Sue Hamilton was working alone in her office. Everyone else had gone home. She had to send an urgent fax, but the office fax machine had broken down and Sue couldn't repair it. So she decided to call the office technician, Jason, to find out how to repair it. She didn't have his telephone number, but luckily she found it on a piece of paper on the office notice board. She called him and when he answered, she began to explain the problem with the fax machine. Before she had finished, he interrupted her:

'Wait. Sue… I'm not at home. I'm in a telephone box. Where did you get the number?'

'What?' she said, 'But I found your number on the notice board!'

'That isn't my phone number! It's my employee tax number, for the accountant.'

'So, what happened?'

'I don't know. I was walking past this phone box when it rang, and I answered it.'

At that moment, he looked down at the number on the telephone. It was identical to his employee number!

Story 3 – The Jigsaw Puzzle

The three clues: 3 - woman in wheelchair; 4 - jigsaw puzzle; 8 - boat on canal

For Christmas 1999, Mr Stuart Spencer received a jigsaw puzzle as a Christmas present from his daughter. It showed a picture of an old boat travelling along a canal in Norfolk, a popular holiday spot in England – about 200 miles from Mr Spencer's home. He started to put it together immediately.

Just as he was finishing the puzzle, he stood back and looked at the picture. Suddenly, he recognised a person sitting in a wheelchair on the boat. It was his wife, Anne, who had died in 1997. The puzzle showed a photograph taken several years before her death when Mr and Mrs Spencer had been in Norfolk and had made several trips together on the boat!

SPEAKING GAMES by Jason Anderson © Delta Publishing 2014

Topic cards (easy)

My favourite food	Yesterday	Dogs
Mobile phones	My family	The Internet
My hobby	This town / city	My favourite TV programme
My first memory	Chocolate	Noisy neighbours
Computer problems	Tomorrow	Dangerous jobs
The English language	Children	Clothes
Designer clothes	Football	This school

Topic cards (challenging)

Pollution	Fast food	Computer viruses
Going to the gym	Politicians	Vegetarians
The person on my left	Dangerous drivers	Giving money to charities
The year 2100	Global warming	My name
Ghosts	Newspapers	People who can't dance
Love	Our teacher	Beggars in the street
My hair	Nelson Mandela	The panda

Word cards

however	banana	with	couldn't	she
he	what	has	crying	were
monkey	which	been	went	did
red	made	wanted	philosopher	the
very	in	movie	ate	stole
friendly	angrily	quite	found	left
lawyer	teacher	chicken	sexy	although
doing	won't	put	criminal	my
read	nurse	nose	despite	asleep

Grammar / Structure Index

Structure	Page No.
1st conditional structures	47, 88
2nd conditional structures	47, 88
3rd conditional structures	56
auxiliary verbs including modal auxiliary verbs	101
both and *neither*	45
can / could for ability	80
cleft sentences	52
comparatives	22, 24, 54
complex sentences	52
conditionals (also see numerals at top of list)	47, 56, 88
conjunctions	10, 83
discourse markers (spoken)	10, 70
future continuous	66
future forms	18, 55, 66, 72
future perfect	66
going to for future intentions / plans	18, 66, 72
have got / have	35
have to for obligation	45
I wish… structures	56
If only… structures	56
indirect speech	60
it as a preparatory subject	52
mixed conditional structures	56
modal verbs (obligation and prohibition)	28
modal verbs (advice)	38
modal verbs (*can, could*)	80
modal verbs (hypothetical)	88, 94
modal verbs (as auxiliary verbs)	101
modal verbs (probability)	102
modal verbs (past deduction)	102, 106
narrative tenses	76, 78, 98, 106, 108
passive forms (present simple, past simple, present perfect)	74

Structure	Page No.
past continuous	16, 76, 98, 102, 106, 108
past modals of deduction	106
past perfect	76, 82, 98, 106, 108
past simple	16, 18, 60, 76, 82, 98, 102, 106, 108
present continuous	102, 108
present continuous for future arrangements	18, 66, 72
present perfect for life experience	78, 80
present simple	14, 64
present simple tense (3rd person)	92
question forms	18, 57, 68, 74, 104
question tags	62
relative clauses	82
reported speech	60
same way question tags	62
sentence formation	82
short answers	101
should have + past participle	56
So do I. / Me too.	42
subordinate clauses	82
superlatives	22
syntax	82
tenses (all tenses / aspects that your learners already know)	40
there is / are	102
time expressions / sequencers	88, 98, 106, 108
used to for past habits	80
verb patterns	55
would, could and *should* to describe hypothetical situations	94
yes / no questions	101
zero conditional structures	50

Topic / Vocabulary Index

Topic / Vocabulary Area	Page No.
adjectives to describe people, places and things	16
adjectives to describe personality	32
animals	24
business	47
clothing	102
countries of the world	20
crime and courtroom	76, 88
drink	68
education	95
expressions for giving opinions	50
features of the face	35
finance	47
food	14, 68
free time activities	20, 104
geography	22
health	14
hobbies	20, 104
idioms	86

Topic / Vocabulary Area	Page No.
jobs	45
language learning	95
linkers	82, 94
parts of speech	26
personal information	57, 64
personal interests	104
phrasal verbs	30
physical appearance	35, 45
relationships	98
science	22
shopping	14, 98
spoken attention signals	42
spoken discourse markers	10, 70
spoken fillers	46
sports	28
suffixes	26
technology	22
tools	90
travel	20

Function / Sub-skill Index

Function / Sub-skill	Page No.
accurately manipulating form at speed	46, 92
adding emphasis	52
agreeing and disagreeing	12, 50, 70, 86
analysing a spoken text critically	60
asking questions	10, 57, 74, 78, 80, 104, 108
asking yes / no questions	35, 101
brainstorming	14, 20, 54, 94
challenging an idea, opinion or the validity of a statement	45, 54, 70
commenting on a topic / issue	52
comparing people, places, things or qualities	22, 24
connecting ideas creatively	82
describing a hobby, a place, the weather, etc.	20
describing abilities	24, 80
describing an image	102
describing appearance	35
describing dishes, food and diets	14
describing future arrangements or plans	18, 66, 72
describing hypothetical situations	94
describing needs, preferences and interests	95
describing past experience, events and habits	74, 78, 80
describing people, places and things	16
describing personality	32
describing procedures	90
describing rules and conditions	28
discussing and coming to a consensus	95
discussing the validity of a statement	22
disputing and justifying opinions	94
drawing comparisons	45
eliciting a chosen answer to a question	101
eliciting agreement	70
explaining an abstract idea	83
expressing feelings and desires	55
expressing obligation and prohibition	28
expressing opinions	12, 50, 52, 70, 86, 88, 95
expressing personal preferences	20
expressing regret and/or criticism	56

Function / Sub-skill	Page No.
formulating a hypothesis	106
formulating questions	18
giving advice	38
giving personal information	14, 104
giving presentations	88, 90
hypothesising about possible abilities, events and habits	80
identifying things in common	66
interrogating a suspect	76
interviewing someone	72
intonation – appropriate use of	42, 62
justifying a suggestion	88, 90
justifying past actions	76
lateral / creative thinking	83
linking ideas together	106
making guesses	62, 108
making predictions	66, 104
making short unprepared speaking turns	60
making suggestions	88
naming items in a list or category	14, 20
narrating a story	16, 98, 106
paraphrasing	64
peer-correcting errors	46, 56
pitching an original business idea	47
predicting	66, 104
predicting the meaning of unfamiliar lexis	86
providing reasons	12, 86, 94
providing short answers to questions	101
recalling an anecdote or information	55, 78
reformulating an idea	64
responding appropriately to news, questions or accusations	30, 42, 47, 57, 76
sequencing ideas	88
showing interest	42
speaking fluently without pausing	10, 46
speculating	66, 106
suggesting	88
telling a story	16, 98, 106
transforming words from one part of speech to another	26
thinking creatively	38, 76